Healing Through Heartbreak: Reflections on *Soul Walk*

G rief lays bare the fragile threads that bind us to the people we love, and in *Soul Walk*, Gina Kitzmiller invites readers into the sacred, shattered space of that unraveling. What begins as a story of youthful love and connection evolves into a brave and unflinching account of her husband's battle with illness, his passing, and the quiet, unsteady march toward healing that follows.

Kitzmiller's prose is lyrical yet grounded, weaving moments of heartbreak with spiritual reflection in a way that feels both deeply personal and universally relatable. Her voice does not hide from the darkness—instead, it walks straight into it. She captures the disorientation of grief with raw vulnerability: the numbness, the longing, the silence left behind. And yet, *Soul Walk* is not a story of despair, but of persistence.

What sets this memoir apart is Kitzmiller's spiritual lens. Through signs, synchronicities, and dream-like connections, she explores how love continues beyond the physical. Her reflections offer comfort for those who believe in something greater and even for those who aren't sure what they believe anymore.

More than a memoir of mourning, *Soul Walk* is a story of survival and rediscovery. It honors the truth that loss doesn't end love, it changes it, shapes it, and ultimately strengthens the one left behind. This book is a gentle companion for anyone navigating grief, a reminder that even in absence, there is presence and even in sorrow, there is soul.

- Ann Collins, Book Reviewer

SOUL WALK

THE UNEXPECTED GIFTS
OF GRIEF & CONNECTION
TO THOSE IN SPIRIT

SOUL WALK

THE UNEXPECTED GIFTS
OF GRIEF & CONNECTION
TO THOSE IN SPIRIT

a memoir

GINA KITZMILLER

ELITE VOICES

ELITE VOICES
San Antonio, TX 78229

First Edition, July 2025
ISBN: 978-1-63765-788-1
Library of Congress Control Number: 2025908802

This memoir reflects the author's personal experiences, memories, and interpretations of events. To respect the privacy of individuals and ensure confidentiality, some names, identifying details, and locations have been changed. Certain events may be recounted through the author's perspective and are not intended to represent the complete or objective truth of those events.

While every effort has been made to present the content with integrity and respect, the narrative is based on the author's recollection and is not intended as a factual representation of all occurrences.

Our mission is to empower individuals and businesses to enhance their professional brand by becoming recognized experts in their field. We provide the tools and resources to help our clients become authors, establish a strong personal brand, and grow their business to achieve greater visibility, credibility, and financial success.

To: Jonah and Jules
I hope you take these broken wings and learn to fly…

Contents

Foreword

On the night of August 26, 2022, I found myself in Columbus, Ohio. I was supposed to be back home in Marietta with my parents, but for the first time in... maybe ever, I asked for space. I packed my son into my sister's car and sent him two hours south while I checked myself into a hotel room—alone.

It was the first night I'd had to myself after my life had burned to the ground.

My marriage had just ended in a spectacular explosion of addiction and betrayal. I was in the ashes, reeling. That night, I sat on the hotel bed and wrote a eulogy for my husband.

He wasn't dead—not technically. But the man I married was gone. His body was still here, but his soul had been hijacked by substances that gutted him from the inside out. It was grief like I'd never known. The kind that drips down your spine and settles into your bones.

After writing the eulogy, I cried one of those silent, body-wracking sobs—the kind that caves in your chest and steals your breath. And then... something shifted. A knowing stirred. A quiet whisper, both unfamiliar and deeply mine, nudged me forward.

I didn't question it. I followed it.

I needed help. Not from a therapist. Not from a friend. From someone who could hold what I didn't have words for.

I opened my laptop and started Googling. I'd never had reiki before—didn't even fully understand what it was. But my spirit knew what my brain didn't. Within minutes, I found a website, and by some small miracle, there was a slot open for the next day.

That's how I met Gina Kitzmiller.

Gina didn't just "do reiki." She held my pain like she'd known it herself. Her presence was grounding, unflinching. I told her about the implosion of my marriage—the infidelity, the addiction, the devastation. And she didn't flinch. Her eyes told me she'd been through her own dark night of the soul. Her hands moved over me and released something I thought would live inside me forever.

At the end of the session, I mentioned I had written a book about my pain, to help others. Her face lit up with true, unfiltered joy—so much joy that I almost cried again. Then she told me she had written one too, about her own experience with loss and healing.

Neither of our books were completely finished. But both of us were holding the first fragile threads of stories we hoped to one day share. And in that moment, I knew: our meeting wasn't random. We were meant to find each other. Two women navigating heartbreak and healing. Two women writing our way out. Two women whispering to ourselves, maybe this pain could become something.

When Gina later sent me the manuscript for *Soul Walk,* I devoured it. I cried through it. I exhaled while reading—those rare, deep exhales that only come when you feel understood on a cellular level. Her story is tender, raw, and fearless. It's spiritual without being preachy, mystical but grounded. It's exactly the book I wish I'd had when I was navigating my own grief.

This isn't just a memoir about loss. It's an invitation—to listen more closely, to trust the invisible, to believe that connection doesn't end when someone dies.

Gina explores what so many people quietly wonder: *Was that a sign from my dad? Did my friend visit me in that dream? Am I allowed to believe in that kind of magic?*

She gives us permission.

She gives us language.

She gives us hope.

Soul Walk is a companion for the moments when your heart breaks open and your old life falls apart. It's a map through grief, yes—but also through intuition, reconnection, and the kind of healing that doesn't erase the pain but transforms it.

Whether you're a suicide loss survivor, someone grieving a parent, or someone wondering what it means when the lights flicker—this book is for you.

And if you're standing in the ashes of your old life, whispering I need help—you've come to the right place.

Keep reading.

Your heart is safe here.

Meredith Beardmore
Author of *Hey Addiction, Thanks for Nothing: A Brutally Honest Guide to Loving an Addict Without Losing Your Mind* and *The Plan B Chronicles: Divorce. Defiance. Liberation.* Creator of *Mend with Mere.*

Chapter 1

"Where are we going?" I asked Joe, for the tenth time. At 17 years-old, we didn't often take scenic drives, especially in Joe's beaten up, rusted Chevrolet. The car heater was broken and the lukewarm air blowing from the vents was no match for the winter chill. My breath fogged up the passenger window as I studied the snow-covered roads, trying to get my bearings. I felt slightly irritated at the cold as I sunk lower into the seat for warmth. Joe and I had just made up from a recent fight and the atmosphere still carried a slight uneasiness between us.

He glanced over at me, his blue eyes nervous.

"I have something special I want to show you," he said offering a small smile, before turning his attention back to the road. "I think this is the right way," he mumbled under his breath, but offered no other information. I watched his face as he scanned the street signs before cautiously turning left on the icy road.

I started throwing out ideas of where we could be going.

"Is it the airport?" I asked.

"No."

"Florida? Are we driving straight to the beach and leaving Ohio behind? Because I'm definitely in," I giggled.

"G, you'll just have to wait and see," he said, pretending to be exasperated. "You have absolutely no patience. You realize that, right?"

"Nope. None." I smiled, pleased the tension between us had broken. I tucked my arm around his and rested my head on his shoulder.

The car slowed as a cemetery entrance came into view. I glanced over at Joe, whose expression was unreadable. Even though I had never been there before, I suddenly knew exactly where we were.

"I wanted to show you how much you mean to me," he said softly, looking over to see my reaction. I found myself at a loss for words.

Joe was in middle school when he lost his older brother, Jeff, in a car accident. His brother was in his early 20's when the tragedy occurred. Despite the age difference, they had been close. Joe said when he was four or five years old, Jeff would let him stay up late and play board games with him. Although Joe shared memories of his brother with me, he rarely opened up about his grief. On one rare occasion, he said that in the year following Jeff's death, he woke up each morning believing it had all been a bad dream.

Joe had not visited the cemetery since the day of the funeral service. He said the loss was too painful to think about, so he mentally closed the chapter and moved forward. Naïvely, I didn't understand why and questioned him about it. However, seeing the cemetery with my own eyes provided a different perspective. 'Jeff' was no longer just a name but a real person. I could picture a young boy approaching the cemetery to say a final goodbye to his big brother. I understood why he might never want to step foot back here and yet he did… the significance of his gesture wasn't lost on me. We sat quietly as the car wound its way through the rolling hills before slowing to a stop.

"Wow, I can't believe I remembered where it was;" Joe said, as he pulled off the road.

I suddenly felt shy as he walked around and opened my door. It was a formal gesture and not typical for a teenage boy. He took my hand and led me up a grassy hill. The memorial stones sparkled around us as sunlight reflected off patches of ice and snow. Joe directed me to the front of a large tree with tangled roots. I noticed the way the dark branches hung starkly against the winter sky.

At the base of the tree, was a memorial stone engraved "Jeff Fairborn June 6, 1968-April 16, 1988." A gold plaque was nailed neatly into the side of the tree with the song title, "Forever Young." I felt unprepared for what to say in that moment and I realized how truly unfamiliar I was with grief; I didn't really understand it.

Joe stood behind me for a few moments. Then he wrapped his arms around my waist and pulled me to him. He buried his head into my hair, and I felt the soft shudder of his body as he silently cried. Standing there, the rest of the world faded to the background, and it was just us: *Gina and Joe.*

I tried to memorize the details of that moment because I knew I would carry it with me. I took in the gentle hills of the cemetery, the tall tree, the winding road and the pond down the lane. Eventually, we turned and walked wordlessly back to the car, holding hands. The colors of the clouds shifted and grew soft with the setting sun. As if on cue, a V formation of geese flew overhead honking loudly against the pink sky. I felt a strange stirring inside; for reasons I couldn't explain, the geese felt significant to me. It felt like a sign; but a sign of what I didn't exactly know.

I had no idea that decades later, I would be standing in that exact spot under the very same tree. Only I would be reading "Joseph P. Kitzmiller 10/10/1975- 10/3/2018" on the plaque, crying until my chest hurt, and desperately trying to make sense of it all.

Chapter 2

"I think my water just broke!" I said breathlessly, trying to move as quickly as I could, cumbersome with my pregnant belly.

"What? Are you sure?" Joe asked me. His eyes scanned me up and down. Despite this being our second child and despite his medical training, we were both slightly panicked.

"I don't know, but I think so! Should I call my parents to come watch Jonah? Where's my hospital bag?"

"I'll call your parents. You get the bag- it's in the spare bedroom."

A short time later, we greeted my parents in the driveway.

"We love you both! Be safe!" my mom said as she rushed over to give each of us a short hug before we scrambled into the car.

"So" Joe said in a light, teasing voice as we drove away, "I see you're wearing your Santa Suit to the hospital then?" He looked sideways and gave me an amused grin. I pretended to give him an angry glare in return. I loved my red velour maternity track suit.

"You know you're going to miss it when this is all done. In fact, I might wear it after the baby's born because it's so comfortable," I taunted him.

Sitting next to the boy I fell in love with at age fifteen, I marveled at the twists and turns life had taken to bring us to that moment.

Joe and I were first introduced briefly in middle school. Back then, Joe's reputation preceded him. He had a big group of friends and was known for breaking the rules. We barely said hello and yet I was immediately curious about this boy with braces and a baseball cap. I shyly watched him with his friends as they goofed around in the driveway, teasing one other.

Two years later, we ran into each other at a high school party. Although I only knew a handful of people, I saw a good-looking guy standing by a pool table and recognized Joe immediately. My stomach flipped at seeing him again.

I deliberately stood close by him so I could start a casual conversation. After a short while, he leaned over and handed me his red plastic cup. I smiled as I took a drink of the bitter tasting beer, before handing it back to him. I began to ask Joe a question but before I could finish we were interrupted by an upper classman who stepped between us and demanded I go hang out with him. I declined the offer, but still the older boy persisted. Not wanting to make a scene, I tried to playfully dodge the advances.

"No chance, Scott." I said, trying to laugh.

"You're coming with me, even if I have to carry you," he responded, attempting to pick me up and carry me.

I started to panic, gripping the pool table with both hands. Joe seemed to read the situation and spoke up.

"I think she's just fine right here. Why don't you go grab another beer?" The older boy eyed him for a long moment then stormed away.

"Sorry about that," Joe said and handed me his cup again.

I was thrilled when Joe offered me a ride home with a group of his friends. Multiple kids were crammed into the tiny car. We were laughing and singing songs loudly the entire way home. As I sat on Joe's lap in the backseat, my cheeks hurt from smiling. After that evening, we began talking every day and quickly fell into a relationship.

Often late at night, we would stay up talking on the phone for hours. I loved our time together while the rest of the house was asleep. In the quiet, it felt like we were the only two people in the world. I briefly examined the orange glow of my cigarette before inhaling. Leaning out the second story window, I blew smoke towards the trees in the front yard. A cool, summer breeze caught the gray smoke and caused it to swirl upwards against a deep purple sky. Gazing at the stars, the night sky felt mysterious and full of possibilities.

"Do you see it yet?" I asked.

"Not yet. *Wait*, there it is. I see it," he said. This was a game we often played at night. We'd tell each other when a plane flew overhead and wait for it to cross the other's house. I smiled as I pictured him lying on the bed by his window.

Even at fifteen, Joe was fearless. In the summer, he would borrow his dad's car at midnight and drive over to my house to tell me goodnight. I never knew what to expect and I loved how daring he was. I would watch from my bedroom window for his car, then quietly tip toe out of the house. We'd drive around or sneak into parks late at night. Joe would bring a blanket and we'd lie under the stars. Away from the confines of my teenage world, this was often the only place I felt free.

One afternoon, we were lying on his bed and talking. He leaned over to light a candle that rested on the windowsill behind the headboard. I saw words carved into the side of the candle as if someone had dug out the wax. I picked it up to examine it more closely.

'I love Gina' was written inside a heart. I felt Joe quietly watching me for a reaction. My heart leapt in my chest. I looked over at him in surprise. I'd been secretly hoping that he was going to tell me he loved me. I'd been trying to lead up to it for days, yet I couldn't make myself take the step and say it first. I was afraid he might not respond the way I wanted.

"When did you do this?" I asked.

"A few days ago," he said. "I wanted you to know how I feel."

"I love you too," I said, with relief, and leaned in to kiss him.

Although we loved each other, we went to different high schools and had different groups of friends. This made it challenging, and we had the dramatic make up and breaks ups of a high school romance. Rumors constantly circled between the two schools, which often caused arguments. It didn't help that I was frequently grounded, causing me to feel isolated and insecure about our relationship. But the break ups never seemed to last long, and we always circled back to each other.

Although we continued to date off and on throughout high school, we both sensed a change during senior year. I had been accepted into a college that was two hours away and would be leaving in the fall. I felt ready to take on the world and wanted new experiences. Joe was all I'd ever known and yet our relationship was complicated. When we were together, it felt perfect; yet when we were apart, we had trouble trusting each other. We frequently pushed each other away out of fear of getting hurt.

A few months before graduation, we sat on Joe's back porch and officially ended our relationship. Old hurts that hadn't been resolved had resurfaced. The relationship had grown strained, and we'd been fighting more frequently. Although we knew we loved each other, the difficulties between us felt like a wall we couldn't break through. Despite our previous breakups, we both sensed something different this time. We sat side by side, tearfully holding hands. We didn't talk for several months afterwards, which was unusual. I stubbornly willed myself forward and tried to ignore the empty space in my life.

Eventually, I reached out to him over the phone from my new dorm room. I was relieved when we began talking like old friends. I told him about my new group of friends at college and my new boyfriend. He told me he was also dating someone. We ended the conversation amicably and agreed to meet the next time I came into town. I was at his house a few weeks later and I met his new girlfriend. To my dismay, I could tell he really liked her. As I made the two-hour drive back to school the following day, I felt conflicted. I tried to push down the feelings of jealousy that tugged at my heart. I tried to have a rational conversation with myself: *Of course, I'm going to feel jealous. It's only natural after dating for so long.* I felt more like myself by the time I finally arrived back on campus. I greeted my friends and began discussing the week ahead. Somehow, it seemed less threatening to have Joe miles away. We remained friends throughout college and made sure to catch up every few months on the phone. Although we both went on to date other people, we still held a connection.

After college, I left Ohio and decided to move to Tampa, Florida. It seemed fitting that I spent my last evening in town with Joe, a few friends and my twin brother, Jason. Once settled in Florida, Joe and I continued to talk regularly on the phone. A few months later, Joe asked to visit me, which caused a big blow up with my boyfriend at the time. I tearfully told Joe he couldn't come and told myself that I was acting like a responsible adult. It wasn't until years later that I learned Joe had planned to 'declare his love' for me on that trip.

Eventually, I relocated to Cleveland, Ohio, while Joe remained a few hours away in Columbus. We began to meet up for lunch and talk more frequently. Despite the distance, I started to think of him romantically. Every time I considered broaching the topic of dating again, I was too afraid to say anything. I worried it would affect our friendship if he didn't feel the same. There were awkward pauses in conversation, where I waited for him to take the lead just as he had in high school. I sensed he had romantic feelings, but he didn't voice them. Just as I thought we might get back together, we both started new relationships and things moved in a different direction. I buried my disappointment and told myself it wouldn't have worked out due to the distance.

Ironically, we both attended each other's first marriage ceremonies in our twenties. My first wedding was a small ceremony of forty people. Although I wanted Joe present, I couldn't explain why I felt uncomfortable seeing him with his fiancée after the ceremony. I was relieved when they said they couldn't stay at the reception. After we got back together, Joe loved to tell people the story of us. He would laugh and say, "I always knew Gina was the one. I almost stood up to object at her wedding, but the priest never said, 'Does anyone object?' It was like he knew!"

My first marriage was brief and ended in my late twenties. My only stipulation in the divorce was to be awarded custody of our yellow Labrador puppy, Bailey. I relocated back to Columbus and settled into a new apartment. Bailey and I spent hours together and he made life a little less lonely. We discovered new walking paths in the evenings and even developed our version of apartment tag, which we played during the winter months.

Even back then, my mom loved to remind me of how well Joe would fit into our family, even though he was already married. When I occasionally saw Joe and his wife, it was uncomfortable. I regretted not telling him how I felt. It was a horrible feeling; knowing the right person was out there but married to someone else. I would try to read his face, hoping for a sign; yet he never said anything. I noticed, though, that he could never fully look me in the eyes, although I wasn't even certain what that meant. I finally came to the realization that I needed to move forward. I continued to date other people and figured I had to learn to accept the loss.

Until the summer when my phone rang in the middle of the night.

"Hello?" I said sleepily.

"Hi…"

"Joe? Is everything OK?" I asked, sitting upright, suddenly wide awake. "Are you there?"

"Tracy and I are separating. We're getting a divorce," he said.

My mind scrambled for an appropriate response.

"I'm so sorry," I said. I remembered how painful a divorce could be and I was sad that Joe would have to go through that experience. However, I also couldn't deny the small flicker of hope that ignited in my heart.

We began talking more frequently on the phone. I was full of anticipation that we might start dating again but I still wasn't sure how he felt so I suggested we meet for dinner. When he agreed, I tore through my closet trying to find the most attractive outfit, finally selecting a white strapless dress with a delicate black print (ignoring the fact it was at least one size too small).

We conversed easily through dinner while sitting on a patio and drinking margaritas. The entire time, I was having an internal dialogue with myself. *Is this a date? It feels like a date. What if he wants to just be friends?*

After dinner, we began walking around the outdoor shopping plaza. When Joe gently took my hand, I was surprised at how natural it felt. My nerves disappeared as we approached a large fountain. Waterspouts splashed in the center of the pool and created a magical feel. Small children leaned dangerously close to the water as they strained for a view of the coins resting on the bottom. Overhead string lights twinkled in the sky and cast a warm glow across the square.

Joe rolled up his pants and sat on the edge of the fountain. He dared me to get in the water and I defiantly pulled up the bottom of my dress and waded in, laughing. The cool, blue water swirled around my knees, and I looked up just in time to see a penny flying through the air at me.

Plink!

It dropped into the water and quickly sunk to the bottom. Another one followed, all the while Joe was laughing to himself.

"Here, G. Make a wish," he said, smiling. I grinned back at him. Secretly, I wished that I could stay in that moment forever.

I slowly waded through the water towards him, stumbling a bit and giggling. It was an odd sensation; walking towards someone from my past and yet seeing him with new eyes. The energy between us was new and yet familiar. I could tell by the look in his eyes that he was thinking the same thing. He caught my hands and pulled me towards him. I rested my forehead on his briefly before kissing him.

Our families and friends were overjoyed when they learned we were back together. People constantly said, 'I always knew it!' when we told them the news. Even my dog, Bailey, welcomed Joe into our lives as if he'd always been there. I'd often find Joe sitting on the front porch wearing his green medical scrubs and playing the guitar while Bailey happily lounged at his feet. Bailey joined us for our daily runs at the park and we even took him canoeing with us.

A year and half later, I was standing in the large, ornate hotel of the Don Cesar in St. Petersburg, Florida. The famous 'Pink Hotel' was decorated for the Christmas season. White candles, lights, and greenery were displayed in the grand lobby. My friend Kelly leaned over to adjust my veil for the tenth time.

"Are you ready?" she smiled, excitedly.

I picked up the back of my gown and we began to walk through the hotel lobby. Hotel guests turned to watch our procession, murmuring between themselves, 'Oh, look at that! She must be getting married'. I overheard someone comment that my white wedding dress with red trim was perfect for a holiday wedding. The wind was unusually strong as we exited the hotel and walked towards the beach. Gray clouds covered the normally blue sky over the gulf waters. The beach was nearly deserted except for a few windsurfers that glided across the chilly waves.

Joe and I took our places under a sheltered area away from the wind. The palms trees swayed wildly as the wind whipped through the leaves. Due to Joe's schedule in his medical residency, we had decided to elope on January 1ˢᵗ. Only one of my close friends, Kelly and her husband, were present. Yet even without a crowd, it felt momentous. Joe fumbled his vows nervously and we both giggled to each other, then relaxed. He slipped a small silver band on my left hand and our eyes met. To me, it felt like the closing scene of a movie when the 'right' couple finally get back together. I knew I was exactly where I wanted to be and with the person I was meant to be with.

As we prepared to welcome our first son later that year, Joe would tease me by saying he liked 'Chubby Gina.' He'd snicker and duck away if I tried to swat at him in pretend retaliation. At night, we'd lie in bed and read out loud from the pregnancy books. Joe would rest his head on my shoulder and gently poke my belly. He'd laugh in amazement when he received a kick in response. We poured over baby name books and tossed out suggestions for weeks. Joe would search for every silly name and pretend he was really considering it, but we came to a decision rather easily – Jonah David Kitzmiller. We waited until we were at my parents' house for dinner to announce the news. My Dad blinked back tears when he realized that his first grandson's middle name was to be David in honor of him.

My pregnancy progressed without issue, and I loved the experience. I even loved the maternity clothes and watching the growth of my expanding belly. Joe was supportive and, secretly, I hoped he'd give up alcohol for the last part of the pregnancy. However, when I suggested it to him one evening at dinner, he laughed and immediately changed the subject. His reaction surprised me, even though I knew how much he seemed to enjoy drinking; he'd been going out more frequently with his friends and staying out late at night. Perhaps I'd expected him to be more generous, somehow. I wanted to say more but I didn't want an argument, so I swallowed the words and hid my disappointment.

I was scheduled to be induced at the end of June, but I felt unprepared. Joe seemed unfazed by the precipice of parenthood and continued with his normal easy-going manner. On the way to the hospital, he asked if we could stop by the McDonald's drive thru for a bite to eat. He weighed my raised eyebrow and decided against it. At the hospital, Joe kept a close watch over me. I assumed the baby would be born shortly after checking in, but the hours ticked by and there was no change in my progress. We encouraged my parents to go home to get some sleep, but my mom insisted they stay close by. A kind, older nurse came in and adjusted my monitor around midnight. She commented that the baby's heart rate was higher than normal.

"It could be a sign of distress," she cautioned. "I'll call your doctor." When she came back, I looked at her expectantly.

"She won't let me adjust your Pitocin. I'm sorry, but we'll just have to see what happens. At this rate, you won't deliver until morning." I could tell she disagreed with my OB's decision and I grew uneasy. Joe was sitting in the chair next to the bed and patted my hand.

"It's fine. They have him on the monitors."

We both settled in for an uncomfortable night.

The next morning the epidural machine started beeping loudly. I started to complain that I could feel pain on one side of my body and Joe grew anxious. He paced the room and kept checking the hallway for a nurse until one finally arrived.

"She's in pain. The epidural isn't working," he told the nurse. I could hear the concern in his voice.

"I'm sorry but there's nothing we can do at this point," the nurse said. "She's going to have to proceed with delivery. The doctor's arrived and she'll be in shortly."

Joe held my hand and coached me during the delivery, but things didn't go as planned.

"You're so close," the doctor said. "Keep pushing!"

"He's stuck, I can feel it! My side's killing me," I whispered to Joe, urgently, while gripping his hand. An oxygen mask was placed over my face, and I felt a wave of nausea and I breathed in the sickly-sweet almond scent.

"Gina, his heart rate is dropping. We need to go ahead with an emergency C-section," the doctor said, calmly.

I looked to Joe for his approval, and he nodded. "They need to get him, sweetie. I'll be right with you the whole time."

As I gave my consent, I glanced over to the side of the room. To my surprise, an entire surgical team was already waiting in the wings. I looked at a row of strangers dressed in full surgical gear and my heart skipped a beat - I realized I was headed into my first surgery. They wheeled me into the theater and draped a green sheet over my stomach so I couldn't see the procedure. Joe kept a firm grip on my hand and gave me updates as to what was happening. I felt pressure in my stomach but no discomfort. Finally, they announced the baby was out.

"They have him! Wait till you see him," Joe said excitedly. He ran over to watch the nurses take the baby's vitals while I kept my eyes on the ceiling and began shaking as a cold chill descended over me.

"I don't feel well," I told the nurse. I clenched my teeth, but my body kept trembling. Heated blankets were placed across my chest, but my symptoms didn't improve. I couldn't believe how far this was from the birth scene I'd imagined. I felt strangely detached from all of it. I gradually became

32

aware of the doctors counting down repeatedly '10, 9, 8, 7...' followed by a pause and then counting again, '10, 9, 8... I noticed how distinctly the atmosphere in the room had changed. Joe was suddenly back at my side, watching the medical staff intensely and I knew something was wrong.

"What's happening?" I asked. For a moment, the question hung in the air. I looked around, trying to figure out what they weren't telling me.

"Your uterus tore during delivery," the doctor responded, curtly, providing no other details.

The room was completely silent. Joe kept a hand on my shoulder with his eyes glued to the doctor. After several tense minutes, they announced the tear was repaired and I was wheeled into the recovery room. Alone in the room, I glared at the hospital wall. It felt like someone had carved out my stomach with a butcher knife. A nurse came in to check my vitals and ask a few questions, to which I responded sharply. I knew she was concerned, but I didn't care; I felt despondent. She left the room and returned a few minutes later with Joe and my mom. I suspected she told them I needed encouragement. Joe took my hand and leaned in to talk quietly to me. I squeezed my eyes shut as tears slid down my cheeks. I overheard the nurse direct another staff member, 'she needs to see the baby as soon as possible'. They moved me into a regular room and a short time later, a nurse arrived to place a wiggling newborn in my arms. By that time, the dark mood had passed. The baby was bigger than I expected and to my surprise, he had a full head of dark hair. I looked up at Joe, who responded with a grin. Because of the complications, I remained in the hospital for five days. Due to my anxiety, I barely let Joe out of my sight. He went home briefly to shower but slept next to my bed for the week without complaint.

Both sides of the family couldn't wait to meet Jonah. It was a special day when my family arrived because Jason brought his newborn daughter who was only six weeks old. My sister Holly's four-year-old daughter looked on in curiosity. My mom's face held a look of pride. She watched all three of her grown children now with children of their own. Because Jason was my twin, it was touching the newborns were so close in age. Joe and Jason had become close over the years, and they laughed as they 'swapped' babies. My dad jumped up to take pictures. Both new dads beamed as they held the infants up to the camera; one in blue and one in pink. I noticed with surprise how Joe handled the babies with such ease.

Once home, it was a slow recovery from surgery. I struggled to adjust to the demands of motherhood and breastfeeding. Joe took an entire month off from his residency program to be available, pitching in wherever help was needed. He placed blankets over me while I napped and took night shifts with the baby. One day, I found him handwashing my underwear in the bathroom sink and burst out laughing. Together, we learned the roles of new parents. Whether it was first baths or trimming infant sized fingernails, Joe was by my side. His support was needed because Jonah had a touch of colic and was difficult to soothe. Family members came over frequently to provide much needed breaks for us. My sister admitted Jonah was a challenging baby and we joked that even the 'Baby Whisperer' had met her match. He demanded to be held constantly and napped only for short intervals. Joe dragged a large speaker into the hallway trailing the cord across the house, thinking the white noise would be helpful. But nothing seemed to work. The only thing that helped Jonah was fresh air and movement. We took turns walking him around the back yard or up and down our small driveway. The older neighbors would wave and give us knowing smiles. Because Jonah was too small for a jogging stroller, Joe would use the large one with the car carrier. He looked ridiculous running down the street with blankets flying out of the stroller, but he didn't seem to mind. Jonah found the experience soothing, and that was all that mattered.

As Jonah got older, we found a used jogging stroller and began to go on runs as a family. Even in the winter, Joe would encourage me to run with him. The three of us would run the neighborhood even in temperatures well under 40 degrees. I placed Jonah in so many layers of clothes that at times, I feared he might overheat despite the cold.

Eventually, I completed my first half marathon when Jonah was small. I had never run over six miles before and I couldn't believe that I could now run thirteen. Joe encouraged me during my training program and never let me get discouraged. He even participated in the race with me and waited to give me a hug after the finish line. As the years went by, we often traveled out of state to run half marathons, using the trips to take a break from our role as parents and reconnect with each other as a couple.

Before Jonah was born, Joe completed a PhD in Biomedical Engineering and finished medical school. We had several discussions about our future and agreed that family was a priority. As a result, he opted out of a Neurology medical residency and began working in academia and medical research. The relaxed work schedule and lighter workload suited him.

We started looking to purchase a home when Jonah was about eight months old. Joe announced that his sister was getting ready to sell her house and he wanted me to consider it.

I could tell he was sentimental; it was located just down the road from the house he grew up in. He eagerly described the neighborhood, and I began to get excited for this next step in our lives. We visited the house a few days later and as I walked into the living room and looked out the back door, I fell in love. It was easy to imagine Jonah running around the backyard and climbing trees in the summertime. However, I was worried because it was out of our price range; it felt like an impossible dream. I tried not to get my hopes up as we discussed our options. A few weeks later, Joe met with his sister, and she graciously lowered the price to help us purchase the house and we couldn't believe our luck.

We celebrated moving into our first home by throwing Jonah a big birthday celebration. We hung a large 1st birthday banner across the fireplace that was framed with helium balloons. The house was crowded with family members talking and laughing. Jonah toddled around and kept pointing to Joe, who was outside at the grill. I walked him down the patio stairs so he could be with his dad. Joe leaned down and took Jonah's hand to steady him. He patiently began walking Jonah around the backyard to explore. It was a touching moment that I captured in a photo. The image came out perfectly, except I couldn't shake my feeling of discomfort when I noticed the beer bottle in Joe's other hand.

Sometime later, as we sat on the patio while Jonah was napping, Joe confessed that prior to Jonah's birth he'd worried that parenting might change our relationship. I was surprised by the confession because he'd never voiced any concerns during my pregnancy, and it made me wonder if there was anything else he hadn't told me. I'd always assumed that we'd shared everything with each other. What else might he be hiding from me?

"But all the clichés about becoming a dad are true," he said. "When I saw him, I was hit by this wave of love. My whole body felt it – it was unlike anything I've ever experienced."

Two and half years later in 2010, we found ourselves on our way to the hospital for the birth of our second child. I was surprised at how relaxed I felt during the drive. Although Jonah's birth was difficult, the doctor assured me that complications were unlikely with my second delivery. I imagined Jonah's response when we returned home with a baby sister and smiled to myself.

Early the next morning, I was taken to the surgical room to prepare for a c-section. Joe was dressed in full scrubs, which always made him look handsome to me. He kept one hand locked in mine as the doctor began surgery. Like the first time, Joe gave me updates on the procedure.

Finally, the doctor announced the birth of our little girl and the room grew quiet as we waited for her first cry. For a long moment there was only silence, then a tiny angry wail filled the room. There was a collective sigh of relief, and everyone started laughing. Joe's eyes twinkled over his surgical mask as he looked at me. Our daughter, Juliet Noel, had arrived safely in the world and Joe rushed over to be the first to hold her.

Chapter 3

Despite the challenges of parenting young children, there was an easiness to being married to Joe. We enjoyed each other's company and rarely fought. But even with his support, I found being a stay-at-home mom lonely at times, so I signed up for a local mom's club. The club holds weekly home playdates as well as meetups in public locations such as libraries or bounce houses.

At my first playdate, a woman in a colorful tie-dyed shirt stepped in front of me with a big smile.

"Hey, I'm Laurel! Sorry, I didn't shower before coming, but I did manage to brush my teeth…" she laughed and shrugged. "Seriously, parenting is hard!" I found myself smiling back, admiring her candor.

To me, Laurel, was a force of nature, her curly brown hair was untamed, just like her extroverted personality. We became friends and being in her bubbly presence made me feel like I was interesting and fun. I also became friends with Whitney, Deb, and Kelley, who made up the rest of our friend group. We had frequent playdates, went to happy hours, and even ran races together. Our friendships deepened when I saw these women didn't care if my house was clean or if I had it all together. With them, I was able to laugh at the messiness of life. Joe encouraged me to spend time with my new friends outside of mom's club events. He loved to hear some of our silly antics. He'd come home from work to find us talking at the kitchen table and would immediately pull up a chair.

"Tell me the latest Mom's Club gossip," he'd say with a grin.

During that time, I felt like we found our niche. Our schedule was filled with cookouts, football parties, and get-togethers. I had a good marriage and great friends. I had finally found my place in the world. I loved hosting parties and in 2012, we held an "End of the World" party to celebrate the end of the Mayan Calendar. I purchased paper sky lanterns online and decorated the house with streamers and bowls of fortune cookies.

"Only you, Gina," Laurel said, as she looked around. "The Kitzmiller's throw the best parties."

"When we do a theme - we go all out," I joked. "Now help me figure out how to unfold these lanterns!"

Towards the end of the evening one of the husband's called out, "Hey, who took my last two beers from the fridge?"

Conversation paused as everyone looked around to find the guilty party, but I already guessed the culprit. Eventually, everyone's eyes landed on Joe, who was still holding the beer in his hand.

"Seriously, Joe! I told you last time to drink your own beer." My friend's husband gave a frustrated laugh.

Joe smiled and shrugged, "Sorry man, we ran out."

"I have extras. Take one of mine," someone offered and conversation resumed. I looked down at my drink, suddenly uncomfortable. I felt Laurel's eyes rest on me briefly with a questioning look, but couldn't bring myself to look at her.

As night fell, the parents gathered in the front yard with

the large, paper lanterns. The neighborhood was filled with laughter as the kids ran through the dark with sparklers dancing in the air. Joe and I giggled as we made a clumsy attempt to expand the four-foot lantern. He held the frame steady while I lit the burner. The lantern emitted a warm glow as it slowly began to rise into the air.

"Make a wish for the end of the world," I joked.

One by one, golden lanterns floated up into the night sky.

"Whoa," the kids exclaimed.

All faces turned towards the stars; the lights were mesmerizing as we watched them float gently into th night sky. There was something almost magical about it.

"Is anyone concerned about a fire hazard?" someone said, breaking the reverie. I realized the lanterns didn't have any specific safety instructions.

"Yeah, on that note maybe we should go back inside," I said, and we began to gather up the supplies.

I had no way of knowing that we were marking an ending of sorts - not for the world but for my life story. The next chapter was already beginning, and it was one I was completely unprepared for.

Chapter 4

As the kids became preschoolers, I noticed that Joe's drinking was gradually increasing. He began to go out more and more with a specific group of guy friends from high school. He would listen to live music or go to a friend's house to play cards. At the end of the night, he'd walk unsteadily in the door or even crawl in if he was too drunk to stand. After a few arguments about drinking and driving, he started staying over at his friend's house more frequently. I found myself parenting more and more on my own, waking the kids up, making breakfast and getting them ready for school by myself.

"Where's Daddy?" they would ask.

"I don't know," I'd reply, with a pit in my stomach. "I'm not sure."

On the way to preschool, I would discreetly look for Joe's car in the neighborhood to piece together where he'd been the night before. When I tried to explain how I felt, his apologies were replaced with defensiveness. He'd point out that his friends' wives didn't have any issues. I struggled between wanting to be perceived as a 'cool' wife and my desire to express frustration at his absences. Although I pretended things were normal, I could sense something was shifting in my marriage. My thoughts began to revolve around how to manage his drinking. I was constantly calculating in my mind: *Is that his third or fourth drink? How's his mood? Is he going out tonight?*

When his behavior didn't improve, I grew desperate to prove his drinking was out of control. I tried every trick I could think of: I yelled, begged, cried, and threw things. Once I even took pictures of him passing out on the kitchen floor, thinking it would spark a response. If only I could be kind enough, firm enough, mean enough - something would open his eyes and he would change. But nothing made a difference. Eventually, I noticed we weren't being invited to as many parties and I knew it was because of the change in his behavior. When he drank, he was no longer fun and lighthearted. He was often moody and argumentative, even with our friends. I felt alone and yet I didn't know how to explain what was happening. When I thought about telling my friends or family, I felt embarrassed. Here I was, an adult, parenting two kids in a dysfunctional home – clearly, I'd done something wrong to be in this situation.

One night, Joe was arrested for disorderly conduct after refusing to leave a bar. I didn't know he was in jail until his dad called the following afternoon.

"I was just checking to make sure Joe got things worked out. I got a call from the jail last night. I think he should be home by this evening," his dad said.

"What are you talking about? Joe's in jail?" I said, incredulously.

There was an awkward pause as he realized his mistake.

"Well yes, something about being at a bar last night and the police were called. I don't know. You two kids work it out," he said before abruptly hanging up the phone.

Joe arrived home, still outraged at being escorted from the bar. He blamed the officer but there were flaws in his story. From the details, I pieced together that the officer offered to take him home, but Joe was argumentative and refused to provide his address. After a few attempts, the officer had no choice but to place him under arrest.

At times, it felt like I was living with an unruly teenager rather than my husband. *Who was this person that hid alcohol in the trunk of his car then claimed it was a friend's and who lied about their whereabouts?* Inside, I was angry, but I was hiding the full extent of my anger. Part of me hoped that it would miraculously resolve on its own.

Jonah was still in preschool when I attended my first Al Anon meeting. Al Anon is a support program similar to Alcoholics Anonymous. Rather than focusing on the alcoholic, Al Anon is for friends and family members affected by another person's drinking. At that point, I had nowhere else to turn. The façade I had carefully constructed in front of family and friends was wearing thin. I was beyond exhausted from trying to act as if I had everything under control. I had gone through every 'if only' scenario just to find myself sitting on a fold out metal chair in a church with a small group of people living with very similar circumstances to my own. At the first meeting, I wasn't sure that I belonged there – I hoped that I didn't, telling myself at the very last moment that it wasn't for me. But as I stood up to make a quick exit, a woman announced the meeting was starting.

"I'd like to welcome you all to Al Anon." Everyone grew quiet and settled into stillness. I sat back down and put my purse under the chair.

"Are there any first-timers here?" she asked, scanning the audience.

I reluctantly put up my hand and raised my eyes to the room. Heads turned in my direction and I felt self-conscious. To my surprise, a warm applause gently broke through the silence. They welcomed me and explained the program before starting the meeting. I learned Al Anon focuses on personal work rather than trying to change the drinker. The discussion that day was centered around how our lives had become unmanageable. It was a topic that I could relate to. As members spoke, I realized how starkly their lives mirrored my own and I was forced to face a truth that I had been running from for months: Joe's issues with alcohol were not going to be temporary. Al Anon was, in fact, where I belonged.

I didn't say a word during the meeting. I sat quietly with tears streaming down my face. I kept wondering to myself: *How did I end up here? This wasn't supposed to happen. What happened to my happy ending?*

As I stood up to leave, an older woman asked to give me a hug. I nodded and allowed myself to be embraced by a stranger. I fought to hold back tears and wondered what was wrong with me; I rarely cried in front of people. She looked at me with knowing eyes and assured me that I'd be OK. Then she took my arm and led me to a table of literature to take home. I'm sure she had seen people like me before, wearing the same shell-shocked expression at the realization the person they loved was an alcoholic.

I didn't want to admit my story had changed, but I began to secretly go to Al Anon every Tuesday morning. The meeting provided childcare, so I'd take the kids' hands and walk them into the church. I could feel compassionate looks of 'Oh look, she has young children,' but everyone would greet us as if it was a normal day.

"Well, hi there! I like your shoes!" An older woman commented to Jules, who beamed with preschooler's pride.

I found comfort in knowing the people in Al Anon understood me in ways that my family and friends did not. They understood the chaos going on in my home without me having to say a word. Joe was becoming increasingly unpredictable when he was drinking. When he was drunk, he'd follow me around the house trying to provoke a fight. If I practiced what I learned in Al Anon and disengaged, it only seemed to fuel his agitation. There were nights when Joe's eyes would gloss over, and I could see he wasn't really *there*. At times, he quoted Revelations from the Bible and talked about becoming a vigilante to rid the world of evil. I began to sleep in the spare bedroom because his erratic behavior made me uneasy, and I wanted to be closer to the kids in case anything happened. I couldn't put my finger on my exact fear, but I felt the need to remain vigilant.

When things showed no sign of improvement, I told my closest friends and family about Joe's drinking. Some acknowledged they had suspected it was an issue, but most didn't understand the depth of the problem. 'Why doesn't he just quit' a few asked. It was a question that I wished I could answer for all of us. After learning about my situation, one of my close friends asked to discontinue our babysitting co-op because she didn't feel comfortable leaving her kids at my home. She said her father was an alcoholic and she had concerns about her children's safety. I found myself nodding, but her words stung, leaving me ashamed and angry. I found myself turning more and more to my older sister, Holly. Her ex-husband was an alcoholic, so she understood what was going on in my home. Years before, when they were married, I didn't understand alcoholism.

"But what do you mean, he *just didn't come home*, how do you not come home from the grocery store?" I remember asking her naively. Now I understood. Joe began to disappear more frequently, and I often called Holly in tears when I didn't know where he was. Even though she never attended Al Anon, she instinctively followed their tenets. She would remind me to focus on what I could control (myself), and to be present for the kids.

It feels odd to describe Joe during this time. Even now, it still seems foreign to me. When he was sober, he was his normal, loving self. He walked the kids to the park, took them swimming, and read bedtime stories. But late at night, his personality often became one of a stranger as his levels of alcohol increased. Joe seemed as baffled by his drinking behavior as I was. I tried to broach the topic, but he was adamant that he wasn't an alcoholic. He reluctantly agreed to attend AA meetings, partially to get me off his back. He began to prescribe himself Buspirone to control his drinking. It would force him to have short windows of sobriety, but it was a band-aid for a much deeper problem.

I tried my best to shield the kids from Joe's drinking, but it became difficult. One day, he called and said he was stopping for take-out at a restaurant close by. He assured me that he wasn't drinking and would be home in twenty minutes. He showed up two hours later when a friend found him incoherent at the bar and insisted on driving him home. When I saw his condition, I hurried to get the kids into their car seats, while trying to distract them. Joe staggered along the side of the house before throwing himself over the backyard fence and passing out on the lawn. I drove around the neighborhood trying to figure out my next move. I felt lost without the safety of my home. In tears, I called Laurel and told her what happened.

"I can't take the kids back there and I can't get a hold of my parents. I don't know what to do." I said, in a frantic voice.

She insisted I go directly to her house, and I agreed, relieved to have a destination and someone to talk to. When I walked in with the kids, she was sitting down to dinner with her family. It turned out that her parents were visiting from out of town. Her father jumped up to make me a plate of food and I could tell she'd filled everyone in on the situation. They kindly asked a few questions about what happened, and I answered honestly, but inside I was humiliated by what my life had turned into.

My increasingly chaotic life was punctuated by the moments of calm when I opened the door of the Church to attend Al Anon. Church had always been a comfortable place for me, being raised Catholic, and attending church every Sunday. As a child, I loved the concept of guardian angels, mystics, and saints. I would eagerly say my prayers at night and ask for their assistance. Al Anon is not religious but they talk about surrendering to a Higher Power, which I desperately needed. I began to talk to God daily, write in my journal, and pray. Admitting that I didn't have control over Joe's drinking took an enormous weight off my shoulders. Al Anon taught me to focus on the present rather than my fears for what *might* occur. I also learned to ask God for what I truly needed in the moment. To my surprise, the practice worked, and my spirituality deepened as a result. I saw that if I kept close to God, I could come through hard things and my prayers did not go unanswered.

One thing I often prayed for was a moment of peace and I eventually found the answer in an unexpected place: on a yoga mat. I'd coincidentally signed up for a beginner yoga class at the local gym and it quickly became my favorite hour of the week. I would silence my phone as I stepped onto the mat and let the rest of the world disappear. Focusing only on the instructor's voice, my mental chatter would subside. It was a much-needed reprieve to the disarray around me.

An air of uneasiness permeated the house. It felt like Joe was driving a car 100mph towards a brick wall with me pleading for him to stop. I continued to try to talk to him, but my concerns fell on deaf ears. As he continued to drink, I could feel the imaginary car gaining momentum. One day a neighbor pulled me aside with a concerned look on her face. I braced myself for what she might say.

"I hate to tell you this, but Joe came over a few days ago, drunk, and wanting beer. Don and I talked to him for a while before realizing he had left the kids home alone. We sent him back as soon as we realized. But Gina, he had no idea. He was completely out of it. We're worried about him. Is he OK?" She asked.

From what I could piece together, Joe had been drinking and forgot that I wasn't home. He left the kids watching TV in the living room to walk to the next-door neighbors' house. He returned an hour or so later when the neighbor sent him home. Jonah wasn't aware of what happened, but Jules had realized that he'd left. When I asked her about it, she appeared more confused than frightened. For weeks after, she repeatedly asked in her little preschool voice, 'Mommy, remember when Daddy left us alone'?

I was upset and tried to lay firmer boundaries with Joe. He agreed to attend AA meetings every week, but I could see he was struggling. That uneasiness grew until one night, he didn't come home from his AA meeting. I tried several times to reach him, but the cell phone went straight to voicemail. Finally,

I decided to try to get some sleep because I was scheduled to start training for a new job the following day. Around midnight, there was a loud banging on the front door. I scrambled down the stairs as quickly as I could with my heart racing. I opened the door to find two police officers standing on my porch.

"Are you Regina Kitzmiller?" they asked, and my stomach dropped. My mind scrambled to predict what they were going to say. *Did something happen to Joe? Was my brother injured in the line of duty?*

"Yes," I said, quickly looking back and forth, trying to read their expressions.

"Your husband has been in a motorcycle accident. He ran off the road about a mile from here and almost hit a tree. He was taken by ambulance to the hospital. I'm sorry, but we can't tell you of his condition."

"Is he OK?" I asked, immediately, before realizing they just told me they couldn't answer this question.

"I can't speak to his condition, Ma'am. You'll need to call the hospital." Their unfriendly demeanor made me suspect Joe had been drinking.

I sprinted upstairs for my cell phone and frantically tried to locate the number to the hospital.

"Hello? I'm calling about Joseph Kitzmiller. He was brought in a short while ago?" I asked.

"Joseph Kitzmiller?" the operator confirmed. I could hear the clicking keys of a computer. "Yes. One moment while I put you through to the Chaplain."

My knees felt weak and I sank onto the bed. *Chaplain?*

The Chaplain came on and explained that Joe was in a stable condition. She ran through a brief list of injuries including bruises and a broken collarbone. According to the police report, he failed to make a turn in the road and drove straight into a line of trees. A nearby neighbor heard the crash and called the police. The Chaplain said that when Joe arrived at the hospital, he appeared intoxicated and was combative with staff. For his safety, they had to sedate and intubate him to complete the necessary scans. I found myself cringing inwardly at the thought.

"Does your husband have a drinking problem?" she asked.

"Yes, he's an alcoholic but he won't admit it," I replied, relieved at her directness. "He was supposed to be at an AA meeting. I don't know what to do- we have two young kids. Do I need to come down there? I start training for a new job tomorrow." I started to panic at the thought of missing my first day of work. *How do I cover with my boss? How could Joe do this to me when he knows that I start my job tomorrow?*

"No. There's no need for you to come down. He's sedated and will most likely sleep through the night. But I assume you'll be looking into treatment options for him." She paused, then added, "You may need to be firm with him about treatment. He'd benefit from a 30-day inpatient program." I immediately felt relieved at the suggestion. *This will force him into a rehab program,* I thought. After months of uncertainty, I felt like I'd been given a direction.

The next day, I began to get phone calls from Joe's friends and family as they learned about the accident. Many began to tell me of their growing concerns about Joe's drinking habits.

One of Joe's friends said in a serious tone, "I've been bartending for years, and I see people drink every day. I'm telling you, Gina, his drinking is different; he's an alcoholic."

I made a conscious decision not to go to the hospital. After months of dysfunction, I had reached my breaking point. The anger that had been brewing inside for months had reached a boil. I wanted Joe to wake up in the hospital bed alone and realize that something needed to change. But when Joe finally called, my hopes fell to the wayside. He immediately launched into a fictional story of the incident.

"Gina, I wasn't driving. I met this guy at the bar and he asked to drive my motorcycle and -"

I cut him off.

"I think you're an alcoholic," I said, steadily, breathing calmly. It might sound odd, but even though Joe attended AA meeting and I went to Al Anon, I never used the label of *alcoholic*. In the past, I had talked around the word, afraid of his reaction. "Your friends and family think you're an alcoholic. You need an inpatient program. You're not welcome home until you are sober. If you cannot stay sober, then I'm done." For the first time in our marriage, I hung up on him.

Despite everything we'd been going through, I'd never mentioned divorce or separation before, and I hoped the significance of my statement wouldn't be lost on him. A few of Joe's friends visited him in the hospital and encouraged him to enter a 30-day inpatient rehab. He remained in the hospital for a few more days, but I refused to speak to him. When he realized he had no other choice, he reluctantly agreed to enter a treatment program.

"Daddy's mind isn't thinking clearly so he's going to stay in a place where doctors can help him," I told the kids the following week. It was hard to explain what was happening in a way they would understand.

At home, we settled into the regular routine and an odd sense of peace came over the house. After a year of hypervigilance, it felt like I could breathe again. I knew Joe was safe in a facility and did not have the constant worry in the back of my mind, wondering what the day would bring. I saw a change in the kids as well - as if they too, felt the shift.

Although I was pleased that he was in rehab, I was still angry. I encouraged the kids to call and send pictures but I refused to speak to Joe, so he mailed handwritten letters, as if we were back in high school. He asked me to forgive him, but I refused. I didn't understand alcoholism and I struggled not to take his actions personally.

A few weeks into the program, he asked to see me and the kids. One sunny afternoon, I walked my preschooler and kindergartner towards a large older building that resembled an old brick dormitory. It was surrounded by large trees ablaze with fall colors of red, orange, and yellow. Jules and Jonah ran ahead laughing and collecting leaves. They were too young to understand, and I tried to smile at them as if this was a normal day. I wanted to stay angry, for it was an easier place to be. When I was angry, I didn't have to feel the deep hurt over our relationship. After checking in, we were led into a community room where families could meet with the residents.

"Daddy!" the kids yelled and ran into Joe's open arms. I hung back and told myself I was going to hold firm, but when Joe looked at me, his blue eyes were clear and sober. Butterflies fluttered in my stomach. It dawned on me that I hadn't seen the real Joe in months, and I realized how much I missed my husband. Standing before me was the man I had so willingly married, and my anger softened. He cautiously took my hand as if trying to gauge my response before enveloping me into a big hug. He gave a sigh of relief when I hugged him back.

"I promise, I won't let it happen again," he whispered. I buried my face in his neck to breathe in the scent of him. At that moment, I sent a silent prayer to God to keep us together. Surely a heartfelt prayer was enough to make it true.

For the first time, Joe admitted that he was an alcoholic and began the long road towards recovery. He completed the 30-day program. We agreed that he would stay with family until I trusted that he was truly sober. He worked hard in his program and attended AA meetings several times a week. He got a sponsor and began working on The Steps. We began to have long talks and slowly, our family began to heal as we spent more time together.

That December, we took the kids to a Christmas tree farm for the first time. Jonah proudly marched through the snow, holding the saw as Joe's helper. Jules gleefully ran ahead to pick the biggest Christmas tree. Afterwards, we spent the afternoon drinking hot chocolate in the giftshop. On the way home, the four of us laughed and sang songs. I caught Joe's eye and smiled as I reached for his hand. My heart felt whole; I had my family back. On Christmas Day, I asked if he'd like to move back in. His eyes lit up and he grabbed me in a fierce hug.

"Oh my God, yes!" he exclaimed, with the biggest smile.

Joe often referred to that first year of sobriety as a 'golden year'. We felt it was a time of second chances. He began to spend more time with the kids, and they got to know him in ways they hadn't before. He would make them breakfast and became more involved in their day-to-day activities. As Joe moved into sobriety, we began counseling to address the issues in our marriage. They weren't easy sessions for either of us. I was still processing anger over his drinking. We discussed deeper issues that we'd previously swept under the rug and often left sessions feeling irritable and raw. I saw for the first time, how much Joe kept inside. I used to pride myself in that we didn't argue over little things like many married couples, but I realized we'd been swallowing our feelings, usually to keep the peace. Yet, even after hard sessions, we always came back to the conclusion that we were in it together. Our marriage slowly began to mend, and I became more confident in his recovery program.

Although our friends were supportive of Joe's sobriety, we were no longer comfortable in social settings. We began to shy away from the cookouts and parties where there would be drinking. Slowly, the invites faded. It was a hard adjustment, but we pulled closer as a couple as a result. We spent more time together, often walking the kids to the park in the evenings or going to restaurants alone. My family adored Joe and wanted to support him. My mom immediately banned alcohol from all family get- togethers, and my siblings readily agreed. Everyone asked how they could help him.

At that time, I continued with my yoga practice and finally admitted to Joe that I had a secret desire to become a yoga teacher. Yoga had become a safe haven for me, and I wanted to share the experience with others. Joe thought it was a great idea and said all the right things to boost my confidence. During the yoga training classes, I began to learn about a variety of topics. In addition to the physical body, we learned about the energy body. One class focused on the body's energy centers, known as chakras. I was immediately fascinated by the subject of energy work.

Months later, Joe and I were in Las Vegas, Nevada for a medical conference. I was excited to meet him towards the end of the conference so we could spend a few days together. On the last day of lectures, he suggested I treat myself to a massage while waiting for him to finish. As I browsed the menu of spa services, I saw Reiki Energy Work listed and decided that I would try reiki for the first time. I stopped by the front desk at the hotel and asked to schedule a reiki session in the spa.

"Oh you should totally meet Athena! She's the best!" the girl at the front desk gushed. "She's normally booked for weeks out but let me see if I can rearrange her schedule to fit you in." She called me back an hour later excited, "I was able to get you in at noon today!"

I wasn't sure what to expect as a woman with very short platinum hair entered the waiting room. She smiled, looking at me with the palest blue eyes I'd ever seen. As I greeted her, I felt an odd sensation that she was looking *through* me. She explained that during reiki, I might feel a sensation such as warmth, or that I might see colors. She also noted it was perfectly normal not to feel anything at all. I laid on the table and closed my eyes. She placed her hands on my head and began the session. To my surprise, it wasn't the out of body experience that I'd imagined. I felt a slight fluttering sensation in my chest but, overall, I just felt extremely peaceful. When I told her this after the session, she nodded with a knowing look.

"You released quite a bit from the heart chakra from past lives," she said, without offering a further explanation. "You might feel a little different today. Drink lots of water."

I left without being sure what to think about the experience. Joe and I grabbed lunch then headed to the Red Rocks for a hike. We climbed over boulders, laughing, and talking effortlessly. Although it wasn't dramatic, I did feel different. The landscape colors appeared more vivid, and my perception felt sharper. I was intrigued and wanted to learn more.

When we returned home, I began to investigate reiki training programs. I was excited to find one close by and surprised when my mom expressed interest too, deciding to sign up for the class as well. I was happy to have company.

We sat next to each other in a small room with about eight other students. After a guided meditation, the teacher asked each student to provide details about their experience.

"I didn't see anything, but I felt a deep love and peace in my heart," my mom said, as she shifted nervously in her seat.

"I was handed a pink rose quartz, I think for my heart," I said. I felt pleased with my answer until the woman after me began to speak. She provided a five-minute description of how archangels descended and cut out her heart in a sacred garden. The next student said she saw Jesus and my eyes widened in surprise. On the way home, my mom and I joked that we needed a 'remedial' reiki course for slow learners.

Although I was disappointed not to have the same level of psychic visuals as other students, I felt different after the first reiki attunement. As I drifted to sleep that night, I saw the silhouette of a man standing next to my bed. He was shimmering with a green and yellow light, and I felt safe. The next night, I dreamed of a pyramid and geometric symbols falling all around me. I heard a voice speak in a foreign language but when I woke up, I couldn't remember what was said. I told Joe about it that morning, unsure of the meaning.

Up until that time, my spiritual life was not something I discussed with many people. When I was little, I could sense other presences and it scared me. I would feel someone was standing in a room watching me when no one was visible. In my bedroom, lights would go off and on randomly. Around age ten, I would hear someone call my name and I'd walk into the next room to ask what my mom needed, only to realize there was no one present. At the time, I wondered if there was something wrong with me.

When I was a teenager, I began to have vivid nightmares about spirits. I'd wake up restless and drenched in sweat. The energy had no form, but it was dark and frightening. I slept with a rosary, prayer card, and crystals under my pillow. I constantly prayed to St. Michael in the early morning hours for protection. When I confessed what was going on to my mom, she surprised me by being sympathetic. I think she could see the exhaustion on my face and would often let me stay home from school if I needed more sleep. Although we tried counseling, no one could explain it. One counselor said it was, 'the good and bad battling it out inside'. But that answer didn't make much sense to me, especially as a fifteen-year-old girl.

When I was around seventeen, when I spoke for the first time directly to an 'earthbound' spirit. I instinctively knew he was a teenage boy who had committed suicide. I gave him a name and would talk out loud to him. Part of me felt like I had an imaginary friend, but I knew on a deeper level he was real; I would sit on the edge of my bed and have conversations with him. There was something about his presence that I found comforting. I could feel his sympathy and kindness towards me. Although I couldn't explain it, it seemed to me that we were helping each other navigate something. As I went through college, I gradually felt inclined to outgrow my spiritual senses and turned away from them. Over time, the nightmares became infrequent. I occasionally read metaphysical books, but I didn't actively pursue new practices. However, all these years later, the reiki classes renewed my interest in the spiritual world. In a reiki session, I learned about my spirit guides. One of my guides told the practitioner that his nickname for me was Lady Bug. He said he had been with me for many lives. I immediately felt safe and trusted my guides completely. Coming from a Catholic background, the concept of spirit guides wasn't a far stretch for me.

I began to have dreams and insights more frequently.

I actively worked on opening my third eye through meditation and prayer (I even rested crystals on my forehead). My spiritual awareness grew until one day, I woke up and sensed something had distinctly changed. I could suddenly *feel* the energy in a way that I had never experienced. I could also sense those in spirit far more clearly than before. Instead of feeling a presence, I would *know* details such as 'there is a 20-year-old guy named Scott sitting in the corner chair and he wants me to reunite him with his dad'. I didn't understand what was happening, although I immediately confessed to Joe what was going on. To my surprise, he simply listened. Part of me worried that he might think I was crazy. But he seemed to accept how I felt about it myself. I was rational; I just had an awareness of things beyond physical reality. Coincidentally, I had recently read a book about assisting earthbound spirits to the light. I began to ask if the spirits needed assistance going to the light. I found that most were coming to me for help. Many were lost, angry, or confused. I counseled them, assisted with energy work, and reconnected them to their loved ones in the light.

I didn't confess my new calling to many people, but I mentioned it during a reiki session with Valerie, who was a seasoned practitioner. I asked if she could confirm what was happening. She paused, then said she saw me standing in the center of a stage in a darkened auditorium. Similar to a concert arena, the crowd was holding up lighters towards the stage. She said this represented the individuals I'd helped, and their families who were thanking me.

"Gina, there are a lot of people! Hundreds if not more… you said you've only been doing this for a few weeks?" She looked at me in surprise.

Pleased to have someone validate my experience, I continued to assist spirits, but the energy in my house became disruptive. It felt like a crowd of strangers were walking around all the time and the air felt unsettled. One night I was reading a book to Jules before bed when a loud bang on the wall startled us both. I dropped the book in surprise. I knew it was a spirit that was trying to get my attention. I rushed to finish putting her to bed, but I was disturbed when I saw a gray silhouette out of the corner of my eye. One evening, I was washing the dishes when a man walked directly past me. I saw him as clearly as any physical object in the room. He glanced at me over his shoulder as he exited my back door while I stood frozen, my mouth agape.

As much as I enjoyed getting clearer information, I felt isolated as I struggled to gain control over my senses. Joe was incredibly supportive during this time, hugging me when I was upset and asking questions without judgment. Most importantly, he seemed to believe me, but even with Joe's support, it was a difficult transition and I felt overwhelmed. My day-to-day life was affected; I no longer enjoyed restaurants or public places. I felt bombarded by different energies which created anxiety. I began to avoid being out in public; even the grocery store felt overwhelming.

After two months, I broke down crying in my car and begged God for help. 'I just can't go on like this,' I sobbed. 'I feel like a crazy person, there must be another way'. Over the next few weeks, my perception changed, and the clarity faded as if someone had turned the volume down. Although I could still sense those in spirit, it was without the prior acuity. I was disappointed to lose some of my intuitive abilities, but I reminded myself that I couldn't have it both ways.

I learned over time to set boundaries with spirits. I performed clearings when it was convenient for me. I continued to study reiki from various sources and learned about automatic writing from an online reiki practitioner. One day, she led a guided meditation to facilitate the process of automatic writing. Once settled, she encouraged participants to write down any thought that entered our minds. I closed my eyes and did as she asked. When we finished, I saw that I had written words like 'love' which didn't impress me because it seemed too predictable. But then I noticed something written in the bottom right-hand corner of the page. I had scribbled: *Keep searching. Peace. Shanti. Shanti. Shanti.* I didn't know what 'shanti' meant or why it was repeated three times, but it felt like something had come through. I looked up the definition and saw it meant 'peace' and I was hooked.

I purchased books with titles like *Accessing the Akashic Records* and *How to Talk to Your Spirit Guides* and began to practice with a notebook. I'd ask a question and intuitively write down the first answer that came into my head. Each notebook that I filled became a spiritual journal for me. The more I opened to the process, the more I received. My rational mind questioned it, but I couldn't deny the deeper wisdom in the responses.

I nicknamed my spirit guides, 'The A-Team' (as in A++ or the cheesy 80's show that I loved as a kid). As our relationship grew, I began to communicate with them regularly. The guides were always supportive and loving. They would point out areas for me to ponder and gently nudge me when needed. They would remind me how much they supported my growth, and they never judged my shortcomings. Sometimes it felt like they were actually excited when I was stuck or having a hard emotion. 'Yes but look at what can you learn here,' they would say, when I complained about difficult life events or people. I also started seeking their guidance for my intuitive development and self-reiki practice, filling notebook after notebook with messages from "The A-Team." These messages became an invaluable resource in my spiritual growth. Over time, Joe grew accustomed to hearing about "my team," and it became natural to include them in our conversations.

The next few years floated by without issue, and we were busy working and parenting young children. But in 2017, I sensed trouble was brewing as Joe became unsettled in recovery. His weekly AA meeting attendance dwindled, and his mood grew brooding. There were weeks where he did little more than get up and go to work.

"You're not going to your AA meeting today after work?" I would ask, trying to sound casual as I packed my work bag.

"No, I have too much to do," he'd reply, his tone often slightly sharper than normal, letting me know not to pursue the conversation.

Early in recovery, Joe told me that every aspect of a recovery program had to be the alcoholic's decision. Family members were not to intervene or make suggestions, so I bit my tongue and tried to ignore my growing concern. It didn't help that I couldn't specifically pinpoint what was wrong because he wasn't actively drinking. I read that an alcoholic can be a 'dry drunk' and behave as if they were drinking even in sobriety. When I tentatively asked about his recovery program, Joe defensively told me he was sober, and I reminded myself that I could not do it for him.

Chapter 5

"Joe, come look at this!" I yelled through the front door. I walked back to gaze at one of the largest moths I had ever seen, basking on the wall of the house. We often saw moths in the fall, but this one was distinct. It was a soft brown color with a large wingspan. I was mesmerized by the intricate white pattern on the wings.

"What is it, hon?" Joe said, as he stepped out of the house with a water bottle in hand. "I'm getting ready to go for a quick bike ride."

"Look at this moth," I said, as I glanced over at him. He was wearing black baggy biking shorts and a red T-shirt.

He walked up behind me and looked over my shoulder.

"Wow, that is huge!" he said, leaning in.

"Look at the markings," I pointed out. "Doesn't that look like a skull on the wings?" I grew slightly uneasy as I inspected the moth closer. *Moths didn't predict death, did they?* I wondered. I couldn't imagine seeing a skull on an animal was a *good* sign. "I wonder if it's letting us know Grandma Helen is going to pass soon." My grandmother was in her nineties and had recently been transferred to a rehabilitation facility. I immediately felt a bit of relief; surely, if it was a sign then that was what it was pointing towards.

"I don't know," Joe said, and shrugged. He was used to me talking about spiritual signs. "It's definitely different, but I don't know. If you're worried, maybe you should go see her soon."

I went back inside and consulted Google. I found an image of a Deadhead moth with a skull on its' wings, but they weren't found anywhere near our region. I walked back out and looked for it again. *Yes, it is still there, and it is definitely a skull pattern...but why is a Deadhead moth on my house?*

I pulled out my journal and asked my guides if this was a sign regarding my grandmother passing away. They indicated that yes, it was partially regarding my grandmother's nearing transition; however, they said it was not just a symbol for her change in life, but also for mine. They told me in vague terms that I was preparing to go into a cocoon and would eventually emerge like the butterfly. I felt confused and even a little annoyed. *What did that even mean? I'm not going into any sort of cocoon,* I told myself. *My life is stable.* We were busy trying to balance married life while working and caring for the kids. Although things had been more difficult with Joe's low moods, I wasn't planning on making any changes. I put my journal away but something about the moth kept nagging at me. It felt like I had been given a code that I couldn't seem to crack.

What did it mean?

Part of the answer came a few weeks later when Joe told me he'd had an alcoholic drink and broken his sobriety. Although I'd felt the relapse coming, I was caught off guard by his confession. His voice broke with emotion, and I knew how hard it must have been to admit. He promised he was going to start back into an active recovery program. I wrapped my arms around him as if to shield him from an invisible attacker.

"I love you, we'll get through it," I assured him. "We'll figure it out."

My mind scrambled to put an emergency recovery plan into place. I made a to-do list in my head: he could attend daily meetings, get a new sponsor, go back to inpatient. But in the days that followed, he didn't make any changes to his recovery program, and I grew concerned. Even more frustrating was that Joe's story began to change as the weeks went by and I heard different versions of the relapse. First he'd told me it had been August, then September, then it had been the U2 concert, then while fishing with the guys. Slowly his behavior began to mirror his days of active drinking. I tried to put my head down and will my way through. I pulled out my Al Anon book, but it didn't bring me the comfort it had in the past and the words fell flat on the page. I had tucked away the memories of Joe's drinking days, but the relapse forced them back to the surface. I kept praying it would pass like a strong summer storm, but weeks went by without improvement.

I met with a local medium, whom I had seen previously for guidance. Although I received communication from my guides, I wanted validation from someone else. We sat down and I found myself confiding about Joe's recent relapse. She said my guides advised me to hold a firm boundary and mentioned a possible marital separation, but I balked at the idea.

"Oh no, I have no intention of leaving," I informed her and shook my head. I couldn't even imagine what a life without Joe would look like – I wasn't going anywhere.

A few days later, I woke up after having a vivid dream. I was in a car with my parents and the kids as it was falling from the sky. Clouds whipped past and the wind howled around the car. In the dream, I frantically scrambled into the backseat to buckle their seatbelts before impact. I woke up just as we hit the ground and shot up in bed, startled by the dream. There was only one message that came into my mind: 'Buckle up. Shit is about to hit the fan'.

Joe was restless that afternoon and I was relieved when he told me that he was going with my brother to dinner and a movie. I hoped that talking to Jason would help ease whatever was bothering him. I could see that he was struggling, and suspected it had to do with sobriety. After he left, I dropped Jules at a friend's house for a sleepover. Jonah and I sat up watching a Marvel movie and eating popcorn. I tucked him into bed and was reading a book when the phone rang.

"Are you up? Joe's drunk- I'm bringing him home," my brother said, in a tight voice.

My brother rarely drank alcohol so I knew he wouldn't have encouraged Joe to drink. My heart sank as I prepared for what was coming next. I was waiting on the front porch when Jason's black truck pulled into the driveway. I could hear muffled arguing as the engine died. Joe stumbled out of the truck and dropped to his knees before pulling himself to stand, holding onto the car door for support. He was so intoxicated he could barely walk. I was stunned as I looked to Jason for an explanation.

"I don't know how it happened," he said. "We were at dinner, and he was fine but then he started acting weird when we were paying the bill. We walked over to see a movie when he was stopped for trying to carry a to-go cup into the theater. I swear I never saw him take a drink. One minute he was sober and the next he was wasted." He looked at me helplessly.

"It's not your fault, I'm sure he was drinking in secret. He probably started before you even had dinner," I said.

"I'm a police officer but I totally missed the signs. Why would I try to get in a movie theater with someone carrying alcohol? Do you know how embarrassing that is?"

Joe angrily made a comment from the driveway, swaying, clearly looking for a fight.

Jason turned swiftly and erupted loudly, "How can you do this to your family? Don't you see what you have? You're going to throw it all away!" Angry tears flooded his eyes.

"You think you're so much better than me…" Joe slurred, lurching forward before falling to his knees.

"It's ok," I said, composed, turning my focus back to Jason. "Can you give me his keys so he can't drive tonight? I'll get him into the house." My calm response triggered something in Jason. He tilted his head and looked at me with new eyes.

"I knew he drank, but I never knew it was like this," he said. "This is what you were dealing with all that time?" I could see him connecting the dots from memories of Joe's stay in rehab.

I nodded and held out my hand for Joe's keys.

"It's ok," I said, firmly. "I'll figure out how to deal with it. I just don't know at the moment." I shook my head and sighed. "He can't do this in front of the kids." We both instinctively looked up at the dark house where nine-year-old Jonah was sleeping.

As I helped Joe inside, he was adamant that he didn't do anything wrong. I went upstairs to leave the argument, trying to block out the sound of him storming around the house. After a while it grew quiet and I tiptoed downstairs, but he wasn't in the living room. Wanting to avoid another fight, I cracked open the garage door and saw a figure lying in the driveway. Joe had passed out face first in a pile of vomit; his glasses tilted off his face at a strange angle. I managed to pull off his sweater and roll him out of the mess. I attempted to wake him up, but he drifted in and out of consciousness. I struggled to get him to move towards the house since I couldn't lift him. Every time I prodded him awake, he would begin swearing at me. It took several minutes to get him inside, while he was calling me every name in the book.

'He's going to be so sorry tomorrow. He'll be mortified that he treated me this way,' I told myself. I finally tucked him away in the front room and placed a trash can by his head. I returned to bed and laid awake, listening to every creak of the house. I quietly checked on Joe and Jonah a few times during the night, terrified that Jonah would find Joe passed out and think he was dead. I fully expected an apology the next morning, but Joe was defiant and refused to take responsibility. I was shocked and hurt when he was angry with *me*.

"How can you act like I did something wrong here? All I did was watch a movie with my son and go to bed," I told him, angrily. Still he refused to apologize.

In that moment, I felt something deep inside me change. A vision flashed through my mind's eye in which a long golden thread broke into two pieces and drifted away. But I was too distraught to give it much thought. Joe left for a few hours and returned acting more rational. I worried about the kids, who were now in elementary school. Years had gone by; they had little, if any, memory of Joe drinking. I explained to Joe that the kids couldn't be on the receiving end of his behavior. I asked him to move out while he worked on his recovery. He reluctantly agreed to a trial separation, then he packed a few bags and left that afternoon.

In most marital separations, I would imagine there is a period of discord in the prior weeks or months, times where friends and family might predict that a separation is coming. Yet there wasn't any preparation for my family. Over the course of a weekend, we went from a normal family of four to a divided home. The suddenness made it more confusing and painful for everyone. I tried to remain hopeful that it would only be temporary.

A few weeks into the separation, I was invited to complete training to become a Reiki Master. I asked my spirit guides and they said the timing was right for me to take this next step. Tentatively, I asked Joe and he readily agreed to watch the kids. During the weekend class, I sat next to a woman named Lori, someone I had never met before. We exchanged a few pleasantries and gradually began talking more as the class progressed.

On the second day, she cautiously leaned toward me and asked, "Can I ask you something?"

"Sure," I replied.

"Is your husband sick or dead? Because I see a ring on your finger, but when I picture your house, I only see you and your kids and I'm confused. I don't feel his energy in the home, but it's light... with just you and the kids - it's a good thing." She watched me closely, her curiosity tempered by hesitation.

I blinked, surprised by her accuracy. "Well, you're sort of right," I said. "My husband's an alcoholic. You don't see him in our home because we separated a few weeks ago, so he's not living with us at the moment." It felt strange to share something so personal with someone I had just met, yet there was something about her that inspired trust. I found myself hoping she would say more.

"That must be it!" she exclaimed, nodding in apparent relief. She didn't elaborate further, leaving me with a faint sense of unease, as though she might be holding something back.

She didn't mention it again, and we completed the training. When I entered the room for the Reiki Master attunement, I was struck by how much it resembled a graduation ceremony. I felt the presence of deceased family members and even my best friend, Kristin, who had passed away in our early thirties. My guides assured me that the attunement would be bestowed by Spirit and encouraged me to take pride in how far I had come. While I was excited to receive the Reiki Master title, an undercurrent of apprehension about my marriage still lingered.

I expected the separation would last several weeks, like the first time, but things unfolded differently. Joe refused to return to the 30-day inpatient treatment program out of fear of repercussions from the medical board. He'd already used the medical board's first bite rule and was mandated to random drug and alcohol testing. He feared he would lose his medical license if they discovered the relapse. He began to attend AA meetings more frequently and met with a sponsor again. Several weeks went by, but we couldn't get back on the same page. Joe expected me to forgive him and let him return home. I wanted so badly for my family to be together, yet every time I thought about going back into an alcoholic home, a voice inside would adamantly say, *No*. But I wasn't ready to move forward with a formal divorce either. We began couples and individual counseling and what followed was one of the most painful chapters in my life. I was stuck in limbo - unable to go back and yet unwilling to move onwards.

It may sound strange, but I pulled away from my close friend group. As an introvert, I retreated inside to process my emotions. I wasn't sure how to explain what I was feeling so I rarely allowed myself to be vulnerable. I would occasionally meet 'the girls' for playdates, but I felt like no one really understood what I was going through. I would occasionally see my friends give each other troubled looks as they struggled to find the right questions to ask me. I was at a loss as to which way to turn so I went deeper into the spiritual side of life. When I needed external guidance, I worked with Sara, a medium, whose sessions helped me find a sense of stability. Joe and I continued to spend time together and talked about our problems. Despite the separation, we still cared for each other. Both of us were hopeful that we would resolve our issues and return to living in the same household.

One day, I came home to find our thirteen-year-old Labrador, Bailey, panting and disoriented. He appeared unsteady on his feet and whined at me anxiously. I opened the back door and helped him get outside. As he tried to make it down to the last step, he lost his balance. I partially caught him with both arms and steered him over to the grass. Once he laid down, it was clear that he couldn't stand on his own.

"It's ok, I've got you. I've got you," I said, repeatedly.

I ran inside to call my dad for help then went back outside where a light snow was starting to fall. I put a blanket over Bailey to keep him warm and stroked his fur. My dad arrived a short time later and together we managed to carry Bailey to the car and drive to the animal emergency room.

"Bailey most likely has a brain tumor," the doctor at the ER said. "I can't tell you how long he has. At some point, he won't be able to walk or recognize you. It could be a few days or weeks and he would need a lot of care. Given his age, euthanasia is an option, but I'll give you a few minutes to think about it."

As she walked out, the room began to spin, and I realized I was on the verge of a panic attack. Just as I was about to tell my dad, the doctor walked back in, and I pulled myself together.

"I'm sorry, but Bailey has just had another seizure. I don't think we need to wait for the neurologist's exam. Given his condition, it might be best to let him go," she said, tenderly. I nodded through my tears and agreed. "We'll give him something to be comfortable. If you'd like to call in any other family members, you can do so now. We'll move you to a special room so you can say goodbye."

I tearfully called Joe and he left work immediately. He arrived just as they were bringing Bailey into a small room that was dimly lit by a table lamp and a candle. My dad and Joe patted Bailey and told him good-bye. I sat with him for a few minutes then asked Joe to tell the nurse that we were ready. As she prepared to give Bailey the injection, I wrapped my arms around him and placed my head next to his. It felt like my heart was breaking.

"You were the best dog ever. I love you so much," I said, softly, as I watched her administer the injection. Then for reasons I couldn't explain, I whispered to him, "try to come back to me."

I felt his heart slow and then stop with a soft thud. I couldn't believe how quickly he was gone. When I stood up, I was surprised; without his spirit animating his body, he no longer looked like my Bailey. Joe stayed close to my side as the three of us walked out of the ER. It felt strange to have arrived a few hours before with my dog, and then to be walking out with only a collar and lead. I felt the sympathetic looks from those in the waiting room. With my tear-stained face and empty leash, it wasn't hard to guess what had happened.

"Mom, do you have pink eye?" Jules asked me a few days later. I was standing at the kitchen counter where I had placed a picture of Bailey and a lit candle. "Your eyes are all red."

"No." I gave a small smile at the suggestion. "I'm just sad."

Although I had tried to prepare myself for Bailey's death, I was overwhelmed by sadness. I missed finding him at the top of the stairs each night, patiently waiting for me to come to bed. When I went to pick up his ashes the following week, I sat in my car for several minutes before I could walk into the hospital. The staff member handed me a small wooden box with his name engraved on a plaque. I placed the box in the center of my dresser where it was visible. I found physical reminders of Bailey comforting. One evening, I was standing at the bathroom vanity, when I saw an energy form in the hallway. It was about Bailey's height and moved tentatively towards me for a second before disappearing. I wasn't sure how to explain it, but hoped it was his way of letting me know he was still with me. For days, I journaled and cried over the loss.

A few weeks later, I surprised everyone by deciding to get a new puppy. It was the first time I made a decision without asking Joe's opinion. If he noticed, he didn't say anything and thanked me for including him. I looked through a long list of available puppies, but one stood out to me. It was a honey-colored lab that resembled Bailey; but what drew me to him was the dog's expression. He was lying on his back on the grass, tongue lolling to the side, with a look on his face that could only be described as joy. I emailed the owner and learned he was still available.

The next day, the four of us drove out to a rural farm in the middle of a snowstorm. Jules and Jonah were beside themselves with excitement. After having a senior dog, this was their first-time bringing home a puppy. We pulled into a small farm and saw a flash of golden fur as a puppy ran across the drive and into a nearby pasture. The kids watched eagerly from the car windows as I approached and placed the little dog into the backseat. They fought over who could hold him until the puppy finally curled up in the middle car seat and fell asleep from exhaustion.

"What should we name him?" I asked, and we tossed out ideas.

"Definitely not Princess. Nice try, Jules," Joe laughed. "What about Benson? Or Benjamin Franklin?"

"Benson. That's funny, but I like it. What do you guys think?" I turned and looked at the kids in the backseat. "We could call him Benny for short." The kids gave their approval.

Joe and I spent the evening trying to manage the chaos of two young kids running around with a new puppy. He helped tuck the kids into bed before returning to his apartment. The puppy was inconsolable during the night, and I ended up sleeping next to the crate. As I lay on the hard floor, it felt strange to be handling something on my own. Part of me felt a sense of accomplishment and part of me simply wanted things to go back to how they were - having someone next to me to take the lead.

Chapter 6

In the start of the new year, Joe announced that he wanted to look at short term apartments. Even though I wasn't surprised, the decision felt painful. I told him that I would help in any way I could. We went together as a family to look at apartments and found one less than a mile from our home. Joe signed a six-month lease and was hopeful he'd be home by the summer. We agreed he would have shared parenting time at his new residence, and stressed to the kids that although they would be living in two homes, we were still a team.

"What do you think about this one, Mom?" Jules asked, as she bounced up and down on a fluffy pink daybed. I looked around the furniture store at a sea of bedroom sets.

"That's really cute, sweetie. But I think there's only two bedrooms in your dad's new apartment, so we'll need to look at bunkbeds. Isn't that something you always wanted?" I tried to give her a smile, but inside I felt emotionally drained.

"Yes! Let's go look at that one, over there!" she said, sprinting off. I glanced at Joe, trying to assess how he was doing. Although I was doing my best to put a positive spin on separate residences, it was exhausting for both of us.

"Are you doing OK?" I asked him, quietly, touching his hand.

"Thanks for coming with me. I don't think I could have done this without you," he said. His eyes filled with tears, and I instinctively squeezed his arm. We sadly turned our attention back to the kids and began to pick out furniture for the second home.

I tried to make the changes upbeat for the kids, so we bought new pajamas and bedroom décor. I helped decorate their new room and made sure Joe had everything they would need to keep things as consistent as possible. We began a shared parenting schedule where Joe would have the kids for overnights a few times a week. I printed calendars for both refrigerators so we could keep track of schedules.

On the outside, I looked like I had it under control but for the first time in my life, I struggled being alone. I'd never been without my children, and it felt like my heart was splitting in two. The first time I dropped them off at Joe's apartment, I returned to an empty house that felt foreign. There were no cartoons playing in the living room, kids chattering, or meals to be made. I found the quiet disconcerting. I sat by myself at the empty kitchen table and cried, heartbroken.

My only constant companion was the new puppy, Benny. I took him for long walks simply to get out of the house. As we walked around the familiar neighborhood, I would look at these beautiful homes and think bitterly to myself, *Why do they get to stay together? I did everything right. Why don't I get to keep my family?* During this time, I continued my spiritual practices of meditation, journaling, and talking to my spirit guides. They encouraged me to process my emotions without judgement, but I was angry. The story of 'Gina and Joe' was all I knew, and it was being ripped away from me.

I suggested we start a family game night on Tuesdays to help us adjust. At the time, the kids loved to play the board game, Sorry. Each week, Jules assigned each family member a color and we played at least one game. The kids loved knocking out other players and yelling 'Sorry'! Typically, Joe would leave for his AA meeting before the second game was finished. Jonah would take over, playing his turn. Afterwards, we'd fill Joe in with the results. The situation was far from ideal, but we tried our best to work through it.

One day Jonah asked to run on the treadmill in the basement. I was listening to the rhythmic pounding of his steps when I heard a loud THUMP and then silence. My ear perked up, and I started towards the door just as Jonah appeared on the steps, crying. He'd fallen on the treadmill and sustained burns on his back from the belt. I immediately called Joe who arrived within minutes to examine him. As the situation resolved, it felt good that we could still work together as a team.

After months of counseling and soul searching, I eventually came to a decision. Joe and I were sitting on the front porch when I told him that I had something to say. He knew what was coming and grabbed my hand and held it tightly in both of his.

"I'm sorry," I whispered, trying to swallow the knot in my throat. "But I told you that I would tell you as soon as I reached a decision."

Part of me still couldn't believe that our marriage was ending in a divorce. We sat side by side on the front porch and cried. Then we began to talk about what would happen moving forward. Through our tears, we agreed that we would still be Team Kitzmiller. We would keep the kids as our priority and talked about how we wanted that to look. We both agreed it was important to still do things as a family. A couple of months later, we took a family trip to Kings Island Amusement Park for Jonah's birthday. The kids were excited to spend the entire day with both of us. We laughed together as we rode the rides and visited the water park. At the end of a perfect day, we decided to play a few carnival games. The fairway was glowing with rainbow-colored lights as the last rays of sun disappeared. To everyone's surprise, I won the ring toss and Jules happily chose my prize - a giant stuffed blue Llama. Afterwards, we watched the night fire-works while eating elephant ears. The kids declared it to be 'the best day ever'. As we drove the two hours home, Joe and I talked amicably about how wonderful the day had been. It had been nice to be together as a family again. I imagined how hard it would be for Joe to return to an empty apartment, so I asked if he'd like to stay over and sleep in Jonah's room. He gave me a grateful smile and said he would like that.

My friends sometimes commented that it was odd that we got along so well during the separation. That isn't to say we didn't have difficulty navigating shared parenting, but we never had the hateful animosity that some couples have towards each other. At the heart of our relationship, was a shared desire to never hurt the other person. In my mind, I thought we'd eventually become good friends and co-parent together. I pictured us sitting beside one another in the stands at football games, cheering for the kids. I knew it would feel strange not to be a couple, but I thought that we'd adjust. In the quiet of my heart, I even held a small fear that I might come to regret my decision.

In hindsight, I look back on the year of our separation and I see more clearly the toll it took on Joe. But I never knew the deeper issues, for he never voiced them. If I had asked, he would have assured me that he was fine, and there was no need to worry. For that was Joe; he was so focused on being the rock for everyone around him that he rarely admitted his own struggles.

Chapter 7

"I don't know, I just have a bad feeling about it. I figured if anyone would understand, you would. Are you feeling anything about the trip, like, with your intuition?" Joe asked, looking at me closely. We were seated at the kitchen table while the kids were playing basketball outside.

"Your trip out West? But it sounded like such a good time. Are you concerned about a possible relapse?" I asked, puzzled. Joe had planned to go in early October to a mountain biking festival in Moab, Utah. "I know people will be drinking but won't you be going with the guys from AA?"

"I don't know," he said, uneasily. "I just have a really bad feeling about it. I feel like something bad's going to happen."

"Well, if you feel strongly about it, think it over. I'm not feeling one way or the other. We loved our trip to Moab, but I guess you should trust your instinct," I said.

I was reluctant to encourage the cancellation of the trip, but it was unlike Joe to feel upset about a planned excursion. Normally, he liked to plan trips, especially those with a physical goal. In the past, he completed half marathons and even a Half Iron Man Triathlon. I thought the time away would be good for him because he'd been under pressure regarding his tenure application at the University. A week or so later, he cancelled the trip and notified the AA group. They tried to get him to reconsider but he was firm in his decision.

As we moved into late Summer, Joe began to request fewer overnights with the kids, which was unusual. Single parenting was difficult, but Joe had been doing it with relative ease. I couldn't figure out the reason for the sudden change. Although he told me he needed more time for AA meetings, I noticed he was struggling to get the kids to and from practice even on days he didn't have a meeting. I thought it was temporary, but a short time later he requested to decrease his parenting time during an official mediation appointment. The Mediator scratched his head and looked confused.

"We don't normally have a parent asking for 30% parenting time," he said, cautiously. "That would be the type of arrangement a judge would issue because of outside circumstances – it's a limited amount of time with the kids."

He glanced over his reading glasses at Joe, and I could tell he was concerned. He paused; then casually suggested Joe take a break in the lobby. Once Joe was gone, the mediator asked me if I knew what was going on, but I shook my head and said that I didn't have an explanation. We agreed to encourage Joe to accept more parenting time with the understanding that I would help more as needed. When Joe returned, we got him to agree to a 40/60 shared parenting plan, but it was a strange conversation. Joe had always been such an involved father; I couldn't understand why it felt like we were suddenly moving backwards. It was as if I had all the puzzle pieces but couldn't fit them together to see the whole picture. I called my brother as I left the office to tell him the details of the meeting and express my frustration. I was hoping, as a single dad, he'd have an explanation, but he was as surprised as I was. We both knew that Joe had been under pressure at work, but it seemed out of character for him. We assumed things would improve in the upcoming months as work settled down.

Over the next few weeks, I tried to keep Joe as involved with the kids as I could. We still held the family game nights, but not as often. We attended Jonah's football games and watched Jules cheer, but at times, Joe seemed distracted. My guides kept telling me how much they loved me and how close they were.

'We are holding you so close right now,' they repeated, to the point where I became alarmed.

"Why do you keep saying that? Is something going to happen?" I finally asked them, uneasily.

I didn't get a response.

A few weeks later, driving on a Friday afternoon in late September, Joe called me. His voice broke as he began to speak, and I could tell he was crying. I had trouble making out his words and, for a moment, I thought one of his parents had died.

"I didn't get tenure, the University denied it. It came down to one vote," he said, angrily. "I could lose my job. I don't know what I'm going to do. If I don't get that NIH grant, I'll be out of a job." He sounded panicked, which was unlike him.

"Joe, they aren't going to get rid of you, you're a doctor!" I said, "And worst case – there are a ton of other jobs that you could do. You don't even know if that's going to happen." I was hoping to appeal to him through logic, but he still seemed troubled. "The kids need you more than a paycheck; they need their dad," I said, firmly, thinking about the shared parenting plan.

"We'll figure it out, I could go back to work full time. We'll cut back and make it work. Maybe you can return to clinical trials - you should talk to James. Didn't you say he wanted you back?"

After a few minutes of talking, Joe took a deep breath, and his voice became steady.

"You're right," he said, sounding more like his normal self. "I'm going to call my AA sponsor and talk to him. I didn't mean to dump this on you. Can you take the kids this weekend so I can have some time?"

I felt conflicted at the change of direction, because I wanted to continue the conversation. After all, I was used to being Joe's main support person. It felt uncomfortable to be suddenly asked to step aside, but I told myself that this is what the AA program was teaching him - healthy ways of coping. That would include leaning on the AA support group during difficult times.

"Yes, of course," I replied, allowing him to take the lead.

I reminded him of the weekend schedule: Jonah had a football game at noon the following day and Jules had her birthday dinner with my parents on Sunday. I suggested that he let me know how he was feeling later that weekend and if he'd attend. He sounded rational when he agreed; he said he was going to call his sponsor then calmly thanked me and hung up the phone.

That was the last conversation I ever had with him.

The following day, I left a voicemail reminding him of the location of Jonah's game. As I sat in the bleachers, I kept an eye on the parking lot because I was hoping to see his car pull in. I even left a second message to tell him where we were seated in the stands, but he never showed. I reminded myself that he didn't commit to attending, but I felt unsettled about it.

"Look Mom! There's a ladybug on your shoulder," Jules exclaimed, as we were walking off the field.

I glanced down at the red and black bug and smiled as it flew away. I took it as a sign that that my guides were holding a supportive hand on my shoulder. Despite the reassurance, I felt a sense of foreboding. I was concerned that Joe was drinking again, and I was worried about what that would mean for our family.

I called him on Sunday to remind him of Jules birthday dinner. I left a voicemail and told him that my parents were looking forward to seeing him. When he didn't respond, I called a third time the following day on Jules' birthday. At this point, I assumed he was drinking and avoiding a confrontation. I told him in the voicemail that I wasn't angry with him and asked him to please call on her birthday. Again, the call was met with silence and my uneasiness continued to grow.

In my journal, I wrote that it felt like the calm before the storm.

Chapter 8

A few years ago, Jason was in a car accident while on duty as a police officer. I received a call before 6am and shortly afterwards was collected by one of my brother's colleagues. I sat nervously in the front seat, lights flashing and sirens screaming as we made our way down a dark and rainy freeway to the hospital. I made small talk with the police officer, while an unspoken question hung in the air: how bad was it? His partner had played down the incident during our brief phone call, but I knew there was more to the story; why else, would they wake me before dawn and send a police escort? I'd never been notified of Jason's work accidents before, much less given a police escort.

At the hospital, we parked and walked quickly to a side door. I thought the officer was simply being polite by escorting me inside, but when he opened the door, I found myself standing in a hallway lined with several police officers in uniform. All eyes turned towards me, and my stomach dropped in disbelief. *Oh my God,* I thought, *I should have called someone to be with me. I shouldn't have done this alone.* An officer provided details of the accident and outlined the current scans being completed. Another officer asked if I wanted a cup of coffee and I found myself nodding. They escorted me to a tiny waiting room, where two officers sat formally on either side of me. I fidgeted with the cardboard coffee cup and tried to remain calm.

In that moment, I felt like a dime had been tossed in the air and how it came down would dictate the course of my life. *Heads, he will live; tails, he will die.* I knew that if it landed on tails, it would be *the* moment where my life split in two - the half before my twin brother died and the half that came after.

After a while, the sergeant told me that Jason was in stable condition and led me to the Trauma Unit. My brother was lying on the hospital bed covered by a thin white sheet. I told him I was there, but he mumbled an incoherent response. I settled into the chair next to the bed and watched him sleep. Fellow police officers would stop in to check on Jason briefly, then leave. One police officer bent his head in silent prayer, then put something on the bed. As soon as he left the room, I leaned over and saw a patch of St. Michael resting on Jason's chest like a protective shield. A doctor came in a few hours later to report that Jason's test results were favorable. Thankfully, my brother survived the accident that day.

On October 3, 2018, I felt the possibility of my life splitting in two again, when I received a phone call from Joe's apartment manager. She said that Joe's neighbors were concerned, and she politely asked if I had spoken to him recently. I explained that I'd not been in contact with him and agreed to allow the police to do a wellness check. A few minutes later, one of Joe's family members called. She was frantic, telling me that his car was parked out front but he wasn't answering the door. For the last few days, I'd been revisiting the lessons from Al Anon and giving Joe space to make his own choices. In my mind, I thought we were entering a new stage of alcoholism, but it never occurred to me that he might hurt himself. Suddenly, I began to wonder if I'd been terribly wrong. *Was it possible Joe could have hurt himself?* I tried to reassure myself that he'd never do that to our kids or to his family. *His mother already lost one son. He would never put her through that again*, I told myself.

To ease my growing anxiety, I began to run through the upcoming schedule. Joe planned to be at Jules' birthday party in three days. She had already decorated the dining room table with unicorn placemats and arranged painting easels with six of her friend's names carefully printed on them with a newly eight-year old's handwriting. In addition, he had just registered to take Jonah to a father-son camp the following weekend. Despite my self-assurances, my stomach began to feel unsettled. *She's being irrational*, I tried to tell myself. *Joe's probably at a friend's house from AA. He could be out for a bike ride or a run. He'll be annoyed if this gets blown out of proportion. He'll be happy that I remained logical.*

After the work meeting ended, I tried to refocus on my computer screen, but my eyes kept wandering to the office window. I stared out at the bright blue sky and wondered: *what if I see a police car pull in the driveway? Is my life going to change into a before and after? Has the dime once again been tossed into the air?*

I didn't have to wait long for the answer. As my cell phone rang, I jumped up from my desk and raised the phone to my ear. Time slowed, then stood still. Before I could utter a word, the screaming on the other end told me which way the dime had landed.

"Are you sure? Is this confirmed?" I asked. My mind raced to put together an alternate ending. *Maybe they just thought he was dead,* I thought, desperately *Maybe he was still breathing. Maybe they could resuscitate him.* "Are you sure? This is confirmed?" I asked again. Part of me wondered why I was using such formal language, but my mind couldn't seem to process information fast enough. Between the wails, I sorted out enough details to realize the truth of the situation.

Joe was gone.

He had committed suicide.

I cried out then threw a hand up to muffle the sound as I thought of the kids downstairs. It felt like there was a vice squeezing my ribcage; I couldn't breathe. I hung up and paced the room, frantically trying to think of my next move. I called my parents and asked them to come, but it was a struggle to speak. I could only get a few words out at a time before having to forcibly draw a breath. I called Jason, who'd been notified by a fellow officer and was already driving towards Joe's apartment.

"Call Holly. She'll know what to do," I told myself, as I fumbled to dial the number. My body started violently shaking. I bent over and wrapped one arm around my waist to try to stop the movement. My teeth began to chatter, and I felt totally out of control of my physical self. When Holly picked up the phone, I started rambling nonsensically. Realizing the situation, she immediately took charge.

"Gina, you need to calm down and pull yourself together for the kids." Her stern voice broke through my hysteria. "They can't see you like this; it'll scare them."

I silently nodded into the phone as though she could see me. I tried to breathe.

"But what do I tell them?" I asked, tearfully. My next actions would imprint upon them for the rest of their lives. I didn't want them to remember me wailing. Holly advised me to tell them no details or wait until I could collect myself better. I hung up, still shaking.

Blindly, I walked down the stairs towards the living room. My stomach clenched as if I might throw up. The kids were sitting on couch, quietly watching the TV. As I entered the room, they looked up expectantly, as if they sensed something was coming. I stood, wringing my hands as I tried to form a cohesive thought. I opened my mouth to speak, but the words stuck in my throat. I closed my mouth then tried again, yet still nothing. The passing seconds felt like an eternity.

Finally, in a voice tight with emotion, I stammered, "Your dad...he passed away. He- he died." My voice sounded high pitched and strained. They asked what happened and I shied away from saying suicide; the word itself was too horrendous to utter aloud.

"I'm not sure," I struggled, unsure of the right response. "It might have to do with alcoholism. His mind wasn't thinking clearly."

To my surprise, they didn't question this; it was as if they instinctively knew that I had no real answers to give them.

"I love you," I said, as I sat down on the coach and hugged them. There were a few tears, but we mostly sat in bewilderment (weeks later, ten-year-old Jonah would remark off handedly to me, 'The minute I saw your face, I knew Dad was dead'). My parents arrived and I felt a quiet protectiveness settle over our house. They sat with the kids and spoke in hushed voices. A short time later, Laurel's silver minivan came flying down the road.

"I wasn't sure if I should come or give you space with your family, but I couldn't just sit home and do nothing, I had to at least come and give you a hug." Her words came out in a rush.

"I'm glad you're here," I said, tearfully, as I gave her a hug.

My priority was to create a safe environment for the kids, and everyone took that cue without me voicing it. Friends and family descended upon the house, but privately came and went. The downstairs filled with the sound of muffled voices and tearful exchanges. I looked outside and observed the row of cars lining the street in front of my house. As I stood looking out the window, Jason and Whitney pulled up at the same time. I thought to myself, *The cavalry has arrived*, for that was how it felt; I was losing the battle, and they were the reinforcements. I watched my brother break down crying as he gave Whitney a hug on the street. He rested his forehead on her shoulder for a minute, then they turned and somberly began walking towards the house.

At forty-two years old, I wasn't prepared to step into this role. I was always the child who could slip into the background while the adults planned a relative's funeral. Laurel googled 'what to do when someone dies' and we began going through the checklist. In bare feet, I paced my cement driveway as we tried to decide what to do. We assumed that his immediate family would notify the extended family, so we focused on who else needed to be notified: his friends, his work, my work, etc. I would pass the phone to Laurel to give the news because I was unable to say the words out loud. I tried to stay focused because I couldn't bear to explore the storm of emotions brewing inside.

I sat at my desk later that evening and stared in disbelief at a post-it note with the funeral home information. My fingers nervously traced the square outline as I tried to take deep breaths. I dialed the number and hung up a few times before I collected myself enough to complete the call. I barely held it together while giving the basic information and my voice shook with emotion. I scheduled an appointment for the following day. I hung up and then stared at the phone, still trying to wrap my head around what had just happened.

Sleep was impossible that night. I tucked both kids into my bed and laid next to them with tears streaming down my face. My mind was in an indescribable state of fear, guilt, and loss. I couldn't stop imagining Joe's last moments in my head. I tossed and turned, trying to escape the images, but they continued to torture me. I felt physical pain in my chest as if my heart had shattered. As I lay there crying, I became aware of someone sitting at the foot of the bed. All my life, I thought stories of departed loved ones coming to visit were magical. I would secretly wait after I lost my best friend or my grandparents, yet I never felt anyone sitting with me. On that night, I just had a quiet knowing that someone had come forward to comfort me. I didn't feel an imprint or even look up in my despair, but I knew someone was present and I was grateful.

Eventually, I gave up trying to sleep and tiptoed downstairs before dawn. I sat on the couch with tears streaming down my face. As I stared blindly into the darkened backyard, I struggled to make sense of what had happened. Gradually, I became aware of tingling on the side of my face, almost as if something had brushed against my skin. I paused and looked around, then felt the sensation again. I wondered if it was Joe, and I began talking out loud to him. My emotions swung wildly from one to another: shock, grief, anger, sadness. After a while, I grew exhausted from the emotions. I went into the bathroom for a tissue and, as I turned to leave, the thought popped into my head that maybe this was a life lesson.

"Well, if *this* is the lesson, then I don't want to *fucking* learn it!" I thought, vehemently.

A swell of anger rose from deep inside. Just as I finished the thought, the rose quartz necklace I wore around my neck exploded. Beads showered around me and pinged loudly on the ceramic tiles; it was shocking in the silence of the house. I froze and stood awe-struck and a little frightened at what had happened.

Later that morning, a small group gathered at the funeral home. My brother and a few of Joe's family members offered to help make the arrangements. I was grateful for the help because I was anxious about the process. We sat with our chairs in a circle as the Funeral Director arrived. After introductions, the Director began asking basic questions about Joe. He asked about hobbies and education, and I slowly settled back in my chair, at least these were questions that I could answer.

"And what are your kids' names?" he asked.

"Jonah David and Juliet Noel." I tried to steady my voice, fiddling with a tissue in my hands.

"Jonah David," he repeated as he jotted down the name. "And Juliet... Noel?" He looked questioningly at the notepad.

"Yes. Juliet Noel," I said.

"Noel?" He looked quizzically around the room.

I repeated it again and glanced at my brother with a questioning look. Was I saying it wrong or something? He looked at me and shrugged as if to say, 'I don't know what the issue is.'

"J-U-L-I-E-T. Noel. N-O-E-L." I spelled it slowly, for a fourth time.

His face suddenly brightened. "Oh," he said with a smile. "I thought you said "Juliet- no 'l' and I couldn't figure out how you wanted me to spell it!"

The tension broke and we had a small laugh at the misunderstanding. The entire process took a few hours as we made selections for the service and burial. We were exhausted by the end of the meeting. I gave the kids a big hug when I walked in the front door.

"We did the best we could," I told my parents, tearfully, over their heads. "I think he'd be pleased."

That night I couldn't sleep and cried as the kids slept peacefully next to me. Close to dawn, I felt a presence enter the room and it felt like I was underwater. A voice cut through my thoughts and said, 'Because of my deep love for you and the children, I will remain with you and guide you for the rest of your lives.' I was comforted but I also felt puzzled. Although the voice was distinctly masculine, it didn't *sound* like Joe's voice. I knew it was him, but I wanted absolute proof.

On the third day, the kids asked to return to school to attend the annual Walk-A-Thon fundraiser. It was a special school event that they looked forward to each year. In place of regular classes, each grade would be assigned a timeslot to leave the building and walk on the school track to raise money. The school provided a DJ for music and families were encouraged to walk with the kids. I agreed, thinking the distraction might be good for them. I walked with them to the bus stop before driving Benny to the kennel, where he'd be boarded for a few days, so I could focus on the upcoming funeral services.

As I drove along the country road, the initial shock began to wear off. I had been running on caffeine and adrenaline, and now grief hit me like a sledgehammer, and I was overcome. I gripped the steering wheel and began screaming in the empty car. I yelled at God, my guides, to anyone, to no one…

"Why? You *told* me I'd happy, but I am NOT happy! I'd never have left if I'd known this was going to happen.

Never!" I started to cry so hard that I began to dry-heave.

To this day, I have never felt an emotion as strong as that. I pulled the car over until I could collect myself, shaking. When I returned home, I called my brother.

"I want to go to the apartment, now," I demanded.

"Gina, the cleaners haven't been there yet. I don't think that's a good idea," he said, in a guarded tone. I could tell he was trying to read my emotional state.

"I don't care, I want to go." I sounded like a defiant child and my voice broke with emotion.

I don't know what I was grasping for. Answers? Something gruesome to punish or shock myself into this new reality? He tried to get me to reconsider, but I wouldn't be persuaded. Reluctantly, he agreed we could go if I took some time to think about it. After an hour, the heightened emotions began to pass. I realized the apartment was only going to bring more pain and my desire to see where Joe died was irrational. I wanted to grasp onto something physical, as if I could pull him back to us by retracing his steps. Part of me still believed I could figure out an alternative ending. I was considering this when the phone rang.

"This is the nurse at the elementary school, I'm calling about Jonah…"

I grabbed my car keys and immediately headed to the school to speak with her.

"He says he's having asthma attacks, but I think it's grief," the nurse whispered to me, as we walked towards the small room where Jonah was resting.

"It's probably just the fall pollen, Buddy," the nurse said, in an upbeat tone as we entered the room. "But maybe you should go home for the day." She gave me a knowing look over his shoulder.

As we walked to the car, I called my parents to come and watch him.

"I don't see why I can't just go home and be by myself," Jonah complained, as we walked to the car. I had called my parents to come watch him.

"You're going to have to wait with me and Jules until Mimi and PapPap get to the house," I said. "I don't think it's a good idea for you to be by yourself right now. We don't know how grief is going to come up. I just want to make sure someone is there in case you need them. I promised Jules I would walk with her and she'll be upset if I don't show up. We'll just walk to the track. You can sit on the side if you want, then I'll take you home."

"But I'm fine. I don't need anyone," he said, angrily.

"Maybe, but when you're an adult and look back, I don't want you to remember me leaving you home alone a few days after your dad died. I think you might say that was bad parenting." I nudged him gently with an elbow, in an attempt to lighten the mood and end the argument.

We joined Jules on the track and Jonah begrudgingly joined us for the last few laps. The three of us walking among a group of cheerful people was surreal. I wasn't quite sure how to behave; part of me wanted to blend in and part of me wanted to cry. Jules took my hand and skipped happily next to me, so I took her cue. I plastered a smile on my face and tried to pretend it was a normal day; but I will always remember the three of us carrying this new tragedy on our shoulders. Occasionally, I would see a look of sympathy from another parent and was grateful my sunglasses shielded my eyes. A parent who knew Joe in high school gave us a look of such sorrow that it took my breath away. I blinked hard and looked away. Walking off the track, I could hear the whispers among some of the parents. We were suddenly *those people* that you hear about being struck by tragedy. I thought how often I'd thanked God that it wasn't me and my family going through trauma. On some level, I'd almost believed we were protected from such loss. Yet now on the other side, it felt like a bad dream. Surely, the universe had made a mistake; I wasn't strong enough to join 'those people' on the other side.

Over the weekend, I took the kids to Joe's parents' house for the first time since receiving the news. I wasn't sure what to expect since we were separated, and I was scared they were going to scream, 'this is all your fault'. Yet his family was nothing but kind to me. The kids walked down to a park with some family members while I stood on the porch with Joe's aunt. I expected her to say 'I'm sorry for your loss' or something along those lines.

Instead, she looked out across the street and said, "You know sometimes life doesn't turn out the way you expect it to." It caught my attention, and I looked over at her, curiously. "How old are you?" she asked.

"I'm forty-two," I replied.

"Oh, you're young! You know, five years from now you could be re-married, with a different life. You could have a husband and stepchildren. You have so many years ahead of you. This will only be one part of it." She turned to look at me.

I wasn't sure how to respond; it seemed impossible I might be happy again, but her words gave me hope. *Where you are today is not where you'll be next year, or in five years*, I said to myself. It would become my mantra over the coming months.

"Hold on to your faith," she said, wisely, and I nodded.

Chapter 9

I can't explain how difficult it is to go from a 'normal' week to coordinating a funeral for the following. My mind struggled to catch up with this new and unwelcome reality. Joe and I never discussed details of our funeral services because we assumed that we had years before it would be necessary. Afterwards, people often asked me how I was able to handle the initial days so gracefully. It wasn't grace as much as shock. When things felt overwhelming, I'd tell myself silently, *'this isn't real anyway'* and keep moving forward. Inside, I quietly believed that I would wake to find it was all just a dream; nothing felt real anymore. At one point, I grabbed the handrail to the stairs and realized I was walking like I was ninety years old; every move was tentative and slow. My body felt fragile, like the bones could shatter at any moment. I thought that my hair was going to turn completely gray overnight, like in a movie. For me, the aftershock of suicide was palpable.

The next few days were a blur, but I realized that I kept seeing monarch butterflies, which was unusual. I remembered seeing monarchs as a child, but they had grown uncommon. It had been years since I last saw one and yet they seemed to be everywhere I turned.

I remarked off handedly to Whitney, "What is *with* all the monarch butterflies this year? They're everywhere!" We were standing in my front yard, and I looked up to see the flash of orange and black in the sky.

"You don't know the symbolism of the monarch when someone dies?" she asked, giving me a questioning look before continuing, "It's a sign of rebirth." We both glanced back up at the pairs of fluttering wings above us.

My friends continued to provide as much support as they could. One day, I came home from running errands to find Laurel on her hands and knees, weeding my flower beds in the front yard.

"You clearly haven't done this in months!" she joked, as we surveyed the number of overgrown weeds. I apologized, feeling embarrassed. "Don't worry," she replied, "This is like therapy for me, and at least I'm doing something to help."

The next day, I saw movement in the backyard. I opened my patio door to find Kelley planting large bushels of yellow and white mums.

"Kelley, these are so beautiful," I said, with tears in my eyes. "But I know you're busy, you don't have to do this."

"I wanted your house to look nice on the day of the service since you'll have family here," she explained. "I stopped at the farmer's market down the road. When I told them who they were for, she said her son went to high school with Joe and she was sorry for your loss. She started filling my car with flowers and only charged me for a few of them. How nice is that?" These small acts of kindness reminded me how much support I truly had.

Even with their support, the thought of attending calling hours and the funeral weighed heavily on me. I couldn't wrap my head around what had happened and the last thing I wanted to do was answer well-meaning questions from others. On the day of calling hours, I felt self-conscious putting on make-up and changing into a dress with flowers on it. It suddenly seemed vain. *What does any of this even matter?* I thought, sharply. As I put on a necklace, my eye caught sight of my wedding ring on my dresser. I debated with myself for a few minutes before placing it on my left hand. I wanted it to be a symbol to Joe of how much I loved him.

In the late afternoon, we gathered in the lobby of the funeral home. Everyone talked in quiet tones before the Director led us down the hallway to a set of closed doors. Once the group had assembled, he asked if we were ready to proceed, then opened the doors. I leaned down and took the kids' hands in mine and walked in first, feeling the eyes of family members follow us. Lining the room were plants, flowers, and handmade posters. The kids and I had made our own posters the day before. Jules drew large bubble letters with the kids nicknames for Joe. The signs read 'Big Daddy Joe' and 'Dadcha' in colored markers. We glued our favorite family pictures around the nicknames. I walked the kids to the front and the three of us stood at a small table. On it held candles, our wedding picture, and Joe's silver urn. I wanted to say something meaningful, but my mind went completely blank. I still couldn't believe I was really standing there.

A large crowd began to gather, and it felt surreal to have everyone offering their condolences. Faces from the past floated before me like a strange dream. I knew my main support group would be there, but I was touched to see people I hadn't seen in several years. An old friend, Jeff, arrived still wearing his medic uniform from a work shift, and extended family members had made a three-hour drive to be there. I tried to push aside the reason for my presence and greet everyone with a smile, but mostly I felt numb. At one point, I retreated to the bathroom for a few minutes as the weight of reality began to settle in.

My spirits lifted when I saw that Valerie, the reiki practitioner, had arrived. As a spiritual friend and teacher, I was eager to ask her about Joe's message. I quickly made my way towards her and gave her a hug. I had kept Joe's message safely tucked away and not discussed it with anyone. I felt fragile, as it had provided me with so much comfort, and finally, someone was here to validate it.

"I think Joe sent me a message," I said, eagerly, leaning towards her. I briefly recounted how I felt a presence and told her the message. I held my breath as I waited for her response. She looked off to the side, as if receiving communication from an unseen place before returning her gaze to mine.

"Oh, that wasn't Joe," she replied, without hesitation.

I was stunned.

"But- but it seemed so real," I stuttered. I felt like a small child as I looked down at my shoes and tried to collect myself. Part of me wanted to re-tell the story, believing I'd missed a key detail that would somehow change her opinion. I felt blindsided by her response and struggled to find my balance. *Did I unknowingly make the whole thing up?*

"No, I'm sorry, but that wasn't him," she said, sympathetically.

"Oh….OK, I guess you must be right, then." I said, feeling dazed.

I politely excused myself to talk to other people, but inside, I was devastated.

That night, I walked barefoot in the front yard trying to ground myself because nothing felt real. I looked up at the expansive night sky and wondered about Joe. *Was he out there?* As I tried to will an answer, a shooting star flashed across the sky. *Is that Joe?* I wondered. Maybe he was sending me a sign from wherever he was, but I couldn't figure out exactly where *he* was.

The day of Joe's funeral, I woke up before sunrise and couldn't get back to sleep. I sat by myself on the couch and tried to prepare for the day ahead. I wished I had someone to talk to, but I didn't know who to call. When it came time to wake the kids up, I found them snuggled next to each other in my bed. I marveled at how soundly they were sleeping despite everything going on. I watched them for a few minutes, not wanting to wake them into the reality this day would bring. Finally, I gently nudged their shoulders.

"Hey guys. It's time to get up. We have the funeral today," I said, softly. They didn't say much, but nodded and started to get ready in the clothes I laid out for them.

My family arrived to take us to the funeral home. The day was warm with golden sunshine and a blue sky. It was a stark contrast to how I felt, as if Mother Nature wanted to mock my grief. We entered the funeral home and took our seats at the front of the room. My brother's pastor spoke first, and I wasn't sure what to expect. He surprised me by walking up and taking a seat on the floor in front of us. I tensed as he spoke to the kids directly about the loss of their dad. I worried they would find it upsetting, but I saw they were listening to him solemnly; unaware the entire room was focused on them.

"Grief is like a broken bone. If you break your arm, you go to the doctor and get a cast, right? It hurts a lot at first but with the cast, it can begin to heal. Well, grief is like that. And the cast is the love and support of your family and friends. Their love will help you heal." It was a beautiful analogy, and I couldn't imagine a more fitting way to describe grief to a child. At the end of the service, two of Joe's friends gave eulogies with a comedic tone. They told story after story of Joe, mostly from high school and college. Through their stories, they brought Joe to life for those that didn't know him back then and I know he would have been laughing along with everyone in the room.

During the funeral service, a family member took a black and white picture of me. When I first saw it, I felt slightly offended because I had no recollection of a photo being taken. But then I was mesmerized by it: she'd captured a moment with my brother glancing back at me with a grin. Jonah was sitting next to him laughing, while I was smiling, Jules on my lap. The picture was striking because it showed the many sides of grief. I also saw the strength I found in my family.

But throughout most of the service, I sat frozen in my seat, afraid to turn around. Emotionally, I was holding on by a rapidly fraying thread. When the service finished, people walked up to give me a hug and offer their condolences. I remained composed until I looked up and saw two close friends from my freshman year of college. I hadn't been in contact with them, yet both had traveled from out of town to be present for me. I couldn't control my tears as I hugged them.

At the cemetery, the limousine pulled up to where Joe was to be buried next to his brother. I found it comforting that his grave would be close to Jeff's memorial. I held the kids' hands as we slowly approached the large tree. My heels sank into the soft grass, and I struggled to keep my balance. I hadn't returned to the cemetery since I was seventeen years old. Now, here I was, trying to find the words to explain to my children this is the place where their dad was going to be buried.

We returned to the white tent for the pastor to recite the final prayers. I struggled to pay attention as my thoughts kept turning to Joe's brother. I couldn't stop thinking that Joe had stood in the same spot as a young boy and felt the same emotions of grief. I felt connected to him in a way I couldn't put into words. I also thought about how life continued after the death of a loved one. *Our children will grow up and visit this place with their own children. Seasons will pass, years will go by*, I thought to myself.

I was reflecting on this when Jules grabbed my arm and said, "Mom, look a butterfly!" I glanced up and sure enough, a monarch was dancing in the breeze along the hillside. I gave her a smile and squeezed her hand in acknowledgement.

After the service, we invited guests back to our house for lunch. It had been a team effort by friends and family. The previous day, my sister and girlfriends came over and cleaned my house and Joe's family organized food. I don't remember being a part of the planning at all. When we walked in from the service, my friends had dishes of food lining the kitchen counters.

"Gina, you must be starved. Why don't you eat?" my mom suggested.

Everyone murmured in agreement and parted so I could make myself a plate. I didn't say anything but walked over to the counter. I leaned over the food and unscrewed the bottle of Baileys liquor. I felt the conversation around me quiet as they watched me fill a large coffee mug and top it with fresh coffee. *Say something to me, I dare you*, I thought, as

I felt their eyes on me. *I buried my husband this morning.* Tears stung my eyes as I turned and walked out of the kitchen, suddenly angry at the world. Immediately my group of friends came into the dining room and protectively surrounded me.

"Are you OK?" Laurel asked.

I nodded tearfully, because I couldn't speak, and I took a drink. She eyed me curiously, and I could tell she was trying to decide what to say.

"Do you need more Baileys, because we'll go get you whatever you want. Seriously. I'll run to the drive thru and get more bottles...or a keg if needed," Laurel joked, to lighten the tension.

My anger disappeared as quickly as it came, and I gave a little laugh at her suggestion. "No, I'm fine really. I'll eat in a little bit, I promise."

My friends gathered around me and began describing the antics of trying to prepare the house for company. Apparently, the vacuum went missing, a dining room chair broke, and they couldn't find the prepared food in the garage and almost ordered pizza. I felt myself softening against their familiar banter.

Later that evening, the last of my friends prepared to leave. As they packed up their belongings, I suddenly felt a wave of panic. The house had been full of people constantly coming and going in preparation for the services. But now that it was over, they would be going back to their families and regular lives. They had given so much to us over the last few days, yet I found myself nervous about being left alone. I suddenly questioned how I was going to parent my kids by myself. *What was I supposed to do now?*

The day after the funeral was Joe's 43rd birthday. I was too emotionally drained to do more than briefly mention it to the kids. That evening, the three of us were gathered in the living room. I was lying down with my eyes closed while the kids watched TV. Suddenly, a loud crash echoed from the kitchen. We all jumped up in fright.

I stood up to see what had fallen, but there was nothing out of place in the kitchen. As I turned to sit back down, the standing lamp by the couch began rocking gently back and forth. The motion grew stronger until it looked like it might topple over. I quickly reached out and steadied it just before it could fall.

When I turned, I saw both kids staring at me, their wide eyes full of questions.

"Maybe it was Benny," I suggested, trying to sound casual. We all looked to find Benny still curled up on the floor, fast asleep.

The kids turned back to me, waiting for another explanation.

"It must be your dad," I shrugged, doing my best to make it sound like a normal occurrence. "Tell him Happy Birthday!"

"Happy Birthday, Daddy!" they exclaimed in unison.

Later that night, I laid awake, wondering if Joe was there and trying to let us know that he was still with us.

Chapter 10

There is a Buddhist prayer that reads, 'For all the ways that I harm, negate, doubt, belittle myself, judge or be unkind to myself through my own confusions, I forgive myself.' In the days after Joe's death, I modified that prayer and said to Joe, 'For all the ways I negated, doubted, or judged you, for all the hurts seen and unseen, I'm sorry'. It repeated constantly in my mind as I was getting the kids ready for school, drying my hair, or even washing the dishes. The guilt over Joe's death was overwhelming. I wondered how I missed the signs that he was struggling. I could tell family and friends they were not to blame, but inwardly, I couldn't give myself the same reprieve. *Everyone must secretly blame me for his death,* I thought. *If I hadn't left our marriage, would he still be here?*

Part of me expected life to stand still after Joe's death, but the activities of day-to-day life resumed. There were dishes to put away, laundry to be folded, and the dog to be walked. Surprisingly, daily walks with Benny became therapeutic. It forced me to leave the house and gave me space away from the kids. Only then did I feel comfortable enough to cry. One day, a wave of grief hit me so hard that I stopped walking mid-step and fought the urge to fall to my knees. *You can't fall on the sidewalk- people will stare! Keep moving*! With effort, I forced my feet to continue to move forward. But most days, I felt Joe's presence walking with me and I grew to look forward to my time 'alone' with him. I would tune in intuitively and catch whispers such as, 'keep the kids first and foremost', but the conversations felt largely one-sided. I would ask question after question, without receiving a definitive answer. Despite the limited interaction, I took comfort in knowing he was close by.

One day while walking, I decided to create a movie of our lives for Joe. In my imagination, I selected my favorite memories and replayed them slowly, one by one, beginning with our introduction, proceeding through the birth of our children and our marriage. I imagined that Joe was able to view the scenes along with me. Although tears streamed down my face, I kept the story playing in my mind's eye. *This is what I would like to remember,* I said to him. *This is how I saw you.*

After the funeral, I was left with the grim task of addressing Joe's belongings in the apartment. The authorities believed his body remained in the apartment for five days after his death and I struggled to come to terms with this reality. Jason had stepped in and independently contacted a catastrophic cleaning company. I was relieved to learn there was someone who could go in and do what I wasn't capable of doing.

"The guy said most of it won't be salvageable," Jason said, choosing his words carefully. "Anything that is plastic, fabric, or wood will have to be thrown out. That means couches, clothes, blankets, pretty much everything."

"Are you sure?" I asked, my heart sinking. The kids considered the apartment a second home and would lose half of their belongings.

"Yes, and Gina," he said, with a slight hesitation. "I have to be honest, the apartment… the smell, well, it's bad." He paused to collect himself. I wanted to throw up. There was no way I could do this. I hung up the phone and burst into tears at the unfairness of it all.

"But what do you mean we can't go to the apartment? Why can't we go?" Jules demanded later that evening.

"Well honey, I just don't think it's a good idea, "I fumbled, while trying to evade her questioning. But she persisted, asking to go.

"I'm not sure the police officers will allow it; it's blocked off right now," I said, immediately kicking myself for bringing up the image of a crime scene.

Still, she was unfazed.

"But why not? I want my stuffed animals and blankets," she said, tears filling her eyes.

"I'll see what I can do. But right now, it's looking doubtful," I replied, and tried to change the subject.

It was a hard conversation to have with them and one of many that I felt unprepared for. Part of their lives had vanished overnight, and I couldn't figure out how to reconcile it for them. That night, I pleaded with God to let them have some of their things, along with Joe's personal belongings. I also prayed for the strength to go into the apartment because I felt incapable. I couldn't imagine packing it alone and I worried I was finally going to crack under the pressure. I was relieved when Jason offered to help. Although a few others asked if they could be of assistance, I didn't want to fall apart in front of anyone besides my brother.

A few days later, Jason checked on the apartment and cautioned me that despite the professional cleaning, it would be difficult. The odor in the apartment was overwhelming and he had to periodically sit outside. We checked our calendars and agreed to clear out the apartment a few days later. The next few nights, I had trouble sleeping. I begged God and Joe to help us. 'I can't do this,' I told them. 'It's too much. I need help.' When the day arrived, I felt dazed as I drove the familiar route to the apartment. My stomach knotted as I followed Jason to the front door. As he opened it, I braced myself then stepped inside. I walked around downstairs, slowly taking in the details. Everything was exactly as Joe had left it: the kid's snacks on the counter, books on the side table and Jules's artwork on the walls. I felt a sharp pain in my chest when I saw Joe's boots lying casually by the stairs, as if he might walk out the front door at any minute.

After taking it in, I looked over at Jason, hesitantly, "I don't smell anything, just chemicals."

We were both surprised and I sent up a silent *thank you* to God and Joe, for making it bearable. Jason went outside to collect the moving boxes and I wondered where I should start. I wasn't emotionally ready to go upstairs, which was where they found Joe's body, and decided instead that the kitchen would be the safest place to begin. I tried not to think as I started cleaning out the refrigerator and cabinets. I moved swiftly and methodically as I labeled boxes and collected trash. Once I finished, I made my way upstairs, to where Jason was packing. He met me in the hallway, watching my face as I approached Joe's bedroom. He gave a small nod and stepped aside to give me privacy. I mentally called in angels before stepping over the threshold to the bedroom. My throat tightened as I looked around the room; part of me wanted to sink to the floor and sob while another part wanted to run far away. The mattresses had been removed, but Joe's shoes were still lined up neatly under the bed. Stacks of sweaters and jeans remained untouched in the closet. A box of photos laid open on the dresser as if someone had recently looked through them. Items that were once familiar to me suddenly felt foreign and I was filled with a deep sense of sadness. Wiping away tears, I reminded myself there was no one else to pack his things and I needed to do this. I took a deep breath and asked Jason to pass me an empty box.

That night, I walked in the front door with an armload of stuffed animals and blankets. Jules squealed in delight and immediately began going through her things. We spread Joe's t-shirts out on the living room floor and the kids took turns picking ones to make memorial blankets. Knowing they would have keepsakes of Joe was nothing short of a miracle to me. I asked, and it had been given.

Back at the apartment the following day, my brother left to take the last load of items to the donation center. I walked aimlessly through the rooms as I awaited his return. I found myself drawn towards Joe's bedroom. My eye caught sight of something triangular taped to the door. As I approached, I realized it was the corner of the suicide note he had left behind. I stared at the small piece of paper in horror before reaching out with a trembling hand to tentatively remove it from the door. My mind struggled to piece together the reality that Joe's hand had touched this slip of paper; he had stood where I was standing and put up that note. Even though the funeral service had passed, his actions were still inconceivable to me.

I wondered if the kids felt the same disbelief. *How can I help them process Joe's death when I can't even make sense of it myself?* I wondered. The Funeral Director had suggested I tell the kids that Joe took his own life, which surprised me. He pointed out some children felt betrayed as adults when they discovered the truth had been hidden from them. He also said they often overheard bits and pieces from family members, which could be confusing. His reasoning made sense, but I didn't know how to approach the kids. Finally, one evening after dinner, I explained that I had more information about their dad's death, and we believed Joe had taken his own life. I did my best to explain that he was suffering from depression, but to my dismay, the conversation took a sharp turn when Jules asked to know the details.

"But *how* did Daddy kill himself?" she demanded.

"You know, I'd rather not say," I said, firmly, hoping she would drop the subject.

"But I want to know. How did he do it?" she asked again. She was visibly getting angry. Again, I declined to give a specific answer. Inside, I frantically tried to recall advice from the parenting books on grief, but they never addressed this scenario. I watched in dismay as she became hysterical.

"Why aren't you telling me? Just tell me!" she yelled, her face turning different shades of red.

I was rapidly losing control over the situation, so I made a split decision and told her as simply and as I could, "Daddy put something over his head so he couldn't breathe and went to sleep. He didn't feel any pain. He just went to sleep."

She immediately quieted down and paused to process this response.

"Oh," she replied, as she turned back towards her coloring activity. All the signs of anger dissipated as quickly as they had arisen. "I thought he cut his head off."

I was too stunned to reply and felt a rush of anger towards Joe. *How could you do this to us? How dare you make me have this conversation with them?*

Prior to Joe's death, I knew very little about how children processed grief. Jonah and Jules began sleeping in my bed at night and it created a safe space. We eventually moved a foam mattress next to my bed and nicknamed it 'the nest'. One child would sleep in bed with me, and we rotated whose turn it was for the nest. Despite the tight quarters, I took comfort in having them close to me. Every night, they would say goodnight to each other before calling out into the dark, 'goodnight daddy!'

I observed subtle changes in their behavior after Joe's death. Jonah began to sleep more than normal and yawned excessively. Jules immersed herself in games on my phone or wanted friends over constantly. Although I tried to find children's books on grief, neither one showed much interest. They delved back into school and activities like things were normal. I was puzzled, but Holly (an elementary teacher) assured me this was normal behavior for children and suggested I give them space. And it wasn't hard to focus my attention elsewhere. In the wake of Joe's death, a million questions surfaced: *Would I be able to pay the mortgage? How do I get health insurance? Were the kids and I going to have to move?* Joe was the breadwinner and his paychecks stopped immediately. I couldn't access the bank accounts until the estate was established by an attorney. I took a few weeks off work, but I was terrified of our financial situation. We had little savings and although we had a life insurance policy, it was unclear if it would be paid under the circumstances. Initially, the insurance company was uncooperative, and a complaint had to be filed with the State for not providing a copy of our policies. Almost every business required the final death certificate, which wouldn't be issued for months. I wanted to jump in bed and pull the cover over my head to escape, but decisions had to be made. I canceled anything I could think of to lower the monthly bills. I asked God for help because I didn't have extra money to do things with the kids to distract them, like go to the movies. My friend, Whitney, came over one afternoon and we sat at my dining room table, drinking tea. She asked how I was doing, and I confessed what was going on financially.

"I'm worried about the kids," I said. "I want to take them out to get their minds off things, but we just can't afford it right now."

She gave me a look of surprise, then her eyes filled with tears. "But didn't you see - online people have donated money for exactly what you're talking about: activities with the kids. I'm going to bring a check over later this week."

"What?" I said, in amazement. "You mean people did that...*for us*?"

With their generosity, I knew the first thing I wanted to address– Jules' canceled birthday party. Each year, Jules planned her birthday months in advance and this past year had been no exception. I knew she'd been disappointed so I decided to organize her a belated surprise. Kelley volunteered to coordinate it since I had so much on my plate. With the donations, we decided to host a party for her at a local kid's cooking school. At the time, Jules loved to watch the Food Network's cooking shows and often pretended to have cooking competitions with her friends. The owner kindly added gift bags for each child after hearing about our situation. On a Sunday afternoon, I told Jules that we were going to an open house at Little Chefs.

"We just walk in and take a tour?" she asked, for the twentieth time, as we pulled into the parking lot. Jonah and I gave each other a knowing smile.

"I'm not sure, I think they're going to have food and demonstrations. It'll be fun," I replied, in an upbeat tone.

I looked to see if she recognized my parents' car in the parking lot as we approached the door, but her face remained neutral as she walked into the building. She hung up her coat and the staff directed her to a darkened back room.

As she stepped inside, the lights came on and several girls jumped out from their hiding places and yelled, "*Surprise,* Jules!"

The group rushed to hug her so enthusiastically that she nearly toppled over. She stood, looking confused for a minute, then her face lit up in a smile.

"But you said this was a food demonstration," she said, once she pieced it together.

"Nope! It's a surprise party. Happy belated birthday," I grinned. Family and friends stood to the side and watched as the girls baked homemade pizzas and tie-dyed cupcakes. Jules smiled shyly as everyone sang her Happy Birthday and I could tell she was secretly pleased. Later that night, I felt guilty as I posted the birthday video on social media. I wanted to share the moment with those who donated, but I felt conflicted. *Were people judging me? Did I have the right to show a happy event so soon after Joe's death?* I wondered if there were unspoken guidelines to follow.

My friends and the community continued to reach out in support in the weeks after Joe's death. Whitney coordinated a meal train, and I was shocked when I saw people had volunteered to bring us meals each week for the next few *months*. The kids and I fell quickly into a weekly routine. On Sundays, Jules would happily announce what dinners we could expect each week, while Jonah would joke that everyone's cooking was better than mine. Being able to sit down with my children for dinner each day was an unexpected gift. It also brought some humor into our life, when one day Jonah informed me that a girl in his class had asked what we wanted for dinner that week.

"What did you say?" I asked, absentmindedly, as I continued to load the dishwasher.

"Steak or crab legs," he responded, proudly.

I paused and looked up, embarrassment washing over me.

"Please tell me you're joking," I said to him. "Steak or crab legs? You're supposed to say, 'tacos or pizza.' Do you know how expensive that is?"

He looked at me and shrugged. "Well, she asked what I wanted."

"Jonah," I said, as I started to correct him then laughed until I had tears in my eyes. "They probably think we're nuts!"

I reached out to the family and explained we didn't expect such an expensive dinner. They laughed about the misunderstanding; but on their assigned evening, Jonah gave me a triumphant smile as he sat at the table and took a big bite of steak.

To be on the receiving end of such generosity from the community was one of the most humbling and beautiful experiences of my life. Prior to Joe's death, I was uncomfortable accepting help from others. Anytime someone asked if they could do something for me, anxiety would arise. 'Oh, that's ok, we're fine,' was my standard reply. Yet for the first time in my life, I couldn't shoulder everything on my own. I began asking for assistance and I was surprised to find that people genuinely wanted to help, even with small tasks. What previously caused anxiety became a network of support. Every time I thought I might truly fall; someone was there to pick me up. People offered to purchase stamps, fix broken furniture, watch the kids, and pick up groceries.

One day I sat working at my desk and looked out the window to see the yard was overgrown. I didn't know how to use the lawnmower because Joe had done the yardwork. I added it to my growing To Do list and sighed to myself, feeling exhausted. That afternoon, I heard a sound outside and I went to the window. I saw one of Joe's high school friends mowing the yard. She hadn't asked but just stepped in to help. Tears of gratitude filled my eyes. The following week, my neighbor started mowing the yard and did so for the rest of the season. I don't remember ever having a conversation about it, they just helped where it was needed.

I purchased a few boxes of thank you cards and asked the kids to join me in filling them out. The thank you card had a bouquet on the front with a formal sentiment of gratitude typed on the inside. We sat quietly working until I glanced up at the pile of cards in front of Jonah and one caught my eye. As I picked it up, I saw that Jonah had written, 'Your #1' and signed his name. I found myself unexpectedly laughing.

"It's not really a 'You're #1' moment, but I see where you were going there," I laughed. Jules and Jonah continued to giggle as we finished the thank you notes.

Each year, my family combined the October birthdays into one large family party. Jason's birthday and mine had passed the week after Joe's. I hadn't felt like celebrating, so I agreed to attend with the family party with the kids, thinking it would be good for us to spend time with family. On the day of the party, I had a difficult morning. My eyes were still swollen that afternoon, and I added extra make-up. Once we arrived at my sister's house, I put on a happy face and tried to make conversation with family members and friends, but I was struggling. My family lit candles on a cake and gathered to sing Happy Birthday to the October birthday group. They cheerfully sang the familiar tune with big smiles, but I felt incredibly sad. I stood there, fighting back tears, and thinking, *'There kids here, do not cry'*. It was the saddest thing to experience, the celebration of life amidst death. I tried to be upbeat for the kids. I even smiled for pictures afterwards, but I felt hollow inside. I was protective of the kids and told myself sternly that Joe's death should not steal their happiness; I wouldn't let it.

On the way home from the birthday party, Jules exclaimed, "Hey Mom, did you see that sign from dad?"

I looked up in the rearview mirror, confused.

"Oh, do you mean that sign? I saw it too," Jonah grinned.

"What are you guys talking about?" I asked, curiously.

"There was a sign back there on the road. It said, 'Dad Jokes Rule,'" Jules giggled. The kids loved to tease Joe about his bad 'dad' jokes, and he loved to tell them the corniest ones to make them cringe.

"It was totally Dad," Jules said, and Jonah nodded in agreement, and I smiled to myself.

I tried to help the kids resume their regular schedules. Jonah had missed several football games. The team was short on players, so I encouraged him to return for the last part of the season. I was touched when Joe's best friend, Chris, showed up at the last few games with his family. It made sitting in the bleachers by myself feel a little less awkward. My dad and Chris attended the final champion-ship game, and although I was happy for the company, it didn't alleviate Joe's absence. Jonah played well and towards the end of the game had a surprise interception. We jumped to our feet, cheering, as he ran the ball down the field, nearly scoring a touchdown. It felt bittersweet. Although it was a close game, Jonah's team lost the championship. The look of defeat on Jonah's face was evident as we congratulated him after the game.

"You played so well! Your dad would've been proud," I said, as I hugged him.

"Yeah Jonah, great game," Chris said.

Jonah gave a non-committal shrug, then turned abruptly and walked off the field ahead of us. We exchanged concerned looks as we followed behind him. When we caught up, I tried to fill in the silence with banter about the game, but it felt scripted because I didn't acknowledge the truth. It wasn't just the loss of the game that Jonah was struggling with, it was the loss of his dad. In that moment, it felt like we were actors saying the 'right' lines, but playing roles in a story we hadn't chosen to be in. I watched Jonah's eyes tear up as the team photo was taken and it broke my heart that I couldn't fix things for him.

In the first month after Joe's death, I was naïve to the power of grief. I told myself that I knew Joe was with me in spirit as if this belief would prevent me from feeling the sorrow and pain of his death. I thought if only I could *understand* grief rationally, I could move through it without feeling it. In looking back, I wanted to be so 'spiritually advanced' that I could avoid feeling loss and pain. I remained partially numb from shock in the initial weeks after Joe's death. Yet as the shock thawed, I fell into the abyss of grief. It felt like being caught in an undertow, unable to breathe, and at risk of drowning any moment. I had nightmares of being surrounded by twenty-foot waves of dark, choppy waters.

As a way of coping, I developed a secret routine. Every day, I walked the kids to the bus stop, then I'd brew a strong cup of coffee and sit down at the kitchen table. I would call Joe forward in spirit and talk to him as if he was seated across from me. I'd tell him news about the kids, admit my fears, or ask questions. Sometimes I grew angry, and sometimes I just sat and cried. But I believed he was with me on those mornings, even if I didn't physically see him. I knew on a deeper level that Joe would never leave us alone to pick up the pieces- it simply wasn't who he was.

Eager for more connection, I made an appointment for a reiki session with Lori. By then, she had a growing reiki practice in a small, rural town about an hour away. As I drove past the green fields and trees, I thought about what weighed on my heart. I was still troubled that Valerie said the message wasn't from Joe. When I arrived, I sat down with Lori and tearfully recounted Joe's message and Valerie's reaction.

"But that *was* Joe," Lori said, adamantly. "Why would she tell you it wasn't? And why would she do that at the funeral home? Oh my God, I'm so mad right now!"

I found her anger comforting.

Lori continued, "When I sat in meditation this morning, he came forward because he knew you were coming in today. He wanted to make sure you knew he was here. His presence feels heavy, not dark but heavy."

"That's exactly how I felt it when I got the message," I said, excited to have confirmation. "It's heavy, right?"

My worries began to fade as I climbed onto the massage table and laid down with a soft blanket covering me. Typically, during reiki sessions, I felt warmth as the energy moved through my body, but I didn't feel anything. Lori played a Native American drumming cd and eventually, I drifted into a meditative state. As I relaxed, I saw Joe standing on the right and my heart leapt in happiness at seeing him. His aura shimmered in beautiful gold and yellow hues and his face held a radiant smile. I felt tingling on my right shoulder and arm. Lori remained quiet during the session, but at the end, she asked me to sit up and handed me a bottle of water.

"That was incredible," she exclaimed, in an excited voice. "You know Joe was here, right? He was standing next to you with a hand on your right shoulder and elbow. Was he tall? Because his aura was huge, and it made him look six-feet tall! He was just glowing."

I was relieved that she perceived him the same way I did. It also explained why I felt the sensation on my right arm, and I smiled at the thought of him standing next to me.

"The energy felt different today," I said. "Do you have any idea why?"

"Your heart chakra is completely blocked. I tried to get energy in but you're blocking it. Joe was trying to send joy into your field, but your guilt is not allowing it in." Her interpretation made sense to me; when I first heard that Joe died, I felt my heart immediately close. Prior to his death, my heart chakra felt light and open, but now it was dull and lifeless. *Is my heart chakra broken?* I wondered. *How do I even fix that?*

"You know," Lori's voice broke through my thoughts. "I saw Joe standing next to you at a wedding. It's not for a few years but you were getting married. He was smiling to show he supported your decision and was happy about it."

I found myself shaking my head in disbelief. The thought of dating and marriage was the furthest thing from my mind.

"Give it time," Lori said, as she gave me a hug. "It's going to take time to heal. He really wants the kids to know he loves them. He said to give them a big hug from him."

As I drove home, the sunlight glinted off the water from the winding river that followed along the road. My heart felt comforted by the knowledge that Joe's message was real. However, I wondered why I had so easily accepted Valerie's opinion rather than trusting my own intuition. I wasn't only angry with her, but I was also angry with myself. It was something that I'd continue to ponder for months.

"Lori and I saw your dad during reiki today," I told the kids that night at dinner. "He looked really happy and sends a big hug to each of you." They immediately looked up and grinned.

Chapter 11

I found myself playing detective after Joe's death trying to try piece together information. I combed through his emails, text messages, anything I could get my hands on, to make sense out of it. Someone suggested that I check the search history on his work laptop, which Jonah had been using. One afternoon, I asked Jonah to hand me the laptop. I didn't think I would find anything significant but thought I'd double-check to be safe. At the last moment, I turned the screen away from Jonah while I performed the search. A few clicks of the mouse and suddenly a list of website searches popped up onto the screen. My stomach dropped as I stared at the results, which included searches for different methods of suicide. I couldn't believe that Joe had typed those words. I checked the dates and quickly realized that he'd been actively suicidal for several months, while I'd had no idea. I tried to cover the look of shock on my face, but Jonah realized something was wrong.

"Mom, what is it?" he asked, as my eyes filled with tears. I tried to collect myself and cleared my throat, searching for the right words.

"Well honey, when someone is suicidal, they might explore different ways to commit suicide," I said, trying to sound matter of fact to hide what I was really feeling. "That's what I'm seeing on your dad's computer. It's not uncommon, but it's upsetting and I'm deleting it."

Afterwards, I was left reeling; I couldn't believe it. *Months? How did I not see it?* It made me incredibly sad and frustrated. After all the support Joe had shown me, I didn't understand why he didn't confide in me. Nothing felt straightforward. I wanted to find a document to give me a rational reason for his suicide, something that would make it make sense; only it didn't exist. What I really wanted was a different outcome and every piece of information ultimately led me back to the moment when Joe chose to take his life. I finally said to him through tears of exhaustion, 'I want so badly to piece this back together for you- to come to a different ending. But no matter what I do, I can't. I can't make this end differently for you'. Part of me will always be devastated by that fact. I couldn't fix his alcoholism, his mental health, what course of treatment he took or didn't take. I couldn't lift the blinders from his eyes those last days when all he saw was an escape. Out of love, I wanted to intercede and do it for him; to make him choose a different decision. In my heart, I still wish I could re-write his story.

I was sad, but also angry. As a parent, I was hurt that he didn't leave long letters to the kids; ones that explained his actions, expressed his deep love for them, or offered an apology. I was envious of others who were able to say their goodbyes to loved ones. I thought to myself, *if I knew that I was leaving my kids, I would write a chapter for every major life event filled with things I wanted them to know.* To me, it felt like a slap in the face.

"Seriously? Did we mean so little to you?" I asked Joe, angrily, one morning. I waited for a response and the thought popped into my mind: 'I will talk to them, I will talk to them through you'. But I didn't understand what that meant.

In the weeks after Joe's death Billy Joel's song, Lullabye (Goodnight My Angel), started playing everywhere I went. I heard it countless times: in the car, in the store, or computer. I wasn't particularly fond of the song, so I usually turned the station. I even wondered if Billy Joel was coming to town for a concert because it was playing so frequently. But one day, I sat at my work desk while Jules was on the floor coloring when it came on again. I remembered the song was about a father and daughter and the light bulb finally went off; Joe was trying to get us to listen to the song.

"Honey, I think your dad wants you to hear this song because it's been following us for the last few weeks and I just realized you're always with me when I hear it," I said.

We sat in silence as the song filled the room. I never realized the song was about a father explaining his death to his daughter. My eyes flooded with tears as I listened to the words about how the daughter would always be a part of him.

"You'll always have this song, Jules. It's special, from your dad to you," I told her, wondering how much an eight-year-old could comprehend.

Yet even with the signs of Joe's presence, there were also harder moments in grief. In November, I found out Joe's memorial plaque hadn't been ordered. I thought it was already completed by another family member and it bothered me to think of his grave unmarked, like we'd forgotten about him. I gathered the kids to look at brochures and wondered how we would afford it. The funeral home had graciously allowed us to defer payment, but the cemetery required it immediately. A few days later, my mom called to tell me that a small inheritance from my grandmother would be placed into my bank account. I realized it was enough to pay for the cemetery plaque. My grandmother adored Joe and I knew she would have been pleased to help. The kids and I chose a bronze plaque with a nature scene including mountains and pine trees that we thought Joe would have liked. I called the cemetery and tried my best to hold it together as I placed the order, but my voice wavered the entire time. The woman asked me if there was a quote I would like to put under his name and I faltered, unprepared for this question. *How did I not think of this part?* How do you put the meaning of someone in a mere sentence? How do you sum up a life in a few words like 'Father, Son, or Husband?' In addition, we were separated so it made it confusing. But mostly I kept thinking: *This is Joe. He wasn't just a title.* I started jotting down ideas and chose 'Always in Our Hearts'. I hung up the phone and buried my head in my hands, sobbing. I remained lost in a cloud of grief for the rest of day.

"Gina, what happened with you this week?" my friend Deb asked, cheerfully, as we sat down for lunch the following day. I glanced around at my group of friends, but I couldn't bring myself to talk about it. How could I listen to their everyday issues and respond with, 'Well, I picked out Joe's cemetery plaque yesterday, so there's that...' What could they possibly say after that? I felt like I was on a different planet. No one could understand how that day broke my heart; picking out the plaque made Joe's death real in ways the funeral hadn't.

The autumn season was a dark and quiet time for me. My mind had trouble accepting the reality of Joe's death.

For weeks, I felt like he was traveling overseas. Sometimes I half believed he was going to walk in the front door, and I would tell him, 'The craziest thing happened while you were gone, we thought you were dead!'. I had frustrating dreams where I was in a crowded room with Joe always facing away from me. I would search for him, to try to talk, but I'd only catch glimpses of him from behind.

This uneasiness continued to build until one day, I felt nudged to formally tell Joe goodbye. I set my intention before I sat down in meditation. I felt Joe become present along with my guides and loved ones. Out loud, I told Joe how proud I was to call him my husband in this life. I was proud of the difficulties he faced growing up and as an adult. Despite the end of our marriage, I couldn't imagine anyone else being the father of my children and I was grateful. I told him all the remarkable qualities he had in life and how much I loved him. Then I pictured him walking into the light to join his brother. The image in my mind was vaguely reminiscent of the scene in Ghost when Patrick Swayze walks into the light at the end of the movie.

I thought it was complete until I felt my guides nudge me and say gently, 'Gina, you have to actually let him go'.

I realized that even in my imagination, I was still holding tightly to his arm. I reluctantly released my grip and let him go. I don't know why it felt different in that moment, but it did. It felt like a doctor had placed a hand on my shoulder and delivered the news of 'he's gone'. The reality sank in, along with a deep sorrow. I dropped to the floor and wailed. The energy in the house quieted after that; the unexplained noises stopped and pictures no longer fell off walls without reason; there was just an emptiness and the room for me to feel my grief.

Chapter 12

As I moved through grief, I grew frustrated whenever I felt sad or alone. I desperately wanted to skip ahead to acceptance. It was like knowing the right answer on a test but not understanding how to arrive at it. As time went by, I felt more lost, and I couldn't see my spiritual path anymore. Instead of turning to faith, my despair grew. *What was I doing? Why did I even care about spiritual lessons?* I felt alone, unsure, and unsupported. In brief moments of clarity, I thought to myself, *you have the tools, but you aren't using them.* However, I remained stuck. One day, I tried to connect in for guidance, but I felt intuitively blocked.

"Where is my path? I need direction and guidance! Why isn't this being given? God, I need you. Where are You in this?" I said, in a raised voice.

I was filled with deep anger: I was angry at life, angry at my lack of ability, angry at my lack of control. I broke down and sobbed in frustration. After feeling sorry for myself, I eventually picked up my journal. I opened its' velvet green cover and turned to a random page. I realized it was dated the day before I found out Joe had died. In the entry, I'd written, 'If a person feels lost it is because they have turned their eyes down so they cannot see God. The Divine cannot be perceived in lack. But if they could raise their eyes, they would see the truth. They would see love and support around them. They would know on every level that God already has them in all ways. Separation is perception, it's simply a mind trick.' I saw the coincidence of the timing – here I was, struggling with this exact issue. Gathering myself, I picked up a pen and turned to a blank page in my notebook, then I began to reconnect with my guides and ask questions. They reminded me that they walked with me in everything, even in grief. As I tuned into my connection with God and my A-Team, I felt a renewed sense of support.

I thought about why I had gotten stuck, and I realized Joe's death caused me to pull away from my spiritual team. In a strange way, the tragedy made me unsure of who to trust. I felt a sense of betrayal and my feelings were hurt. I knew my guides were aware this event was going to happen and yet no one had warned me. I felt like everyone else in the room had been in on a big secret, except me. I asked them countless times, 'why didn't you tell me this was going to happen?'. My guides said that everything was done out of great love on my behalf. They reminded me that the marital separation prepared me for Joe's suicide without my knowledge. I was given time to become independent and a single parent, so I was better prepared. As I read books on suicide, I realized some stories were even more horrific than mine. What I experienced was not violent or carried out in front of our children. I realized if Joe had been living with us, the ending could have played out very differently. I was told what I needed to know in the moment, but it took much more soul searching to come to peace with it.

As we moved past Thanksgiving into the Christmas season, I tried to put one foot in front of the other. I was familiar with the saying 'one step forward, two steps back', but grief felt like 'one step forward, ten steps backward'. Although the waves of grief were still coming regularly, eventually, I began to have small windows of reprieve. Some breaks lasted a few hours, sometimes a whole day. My guides kept a steady hand on my shoulder, and I sat in quiet contemplation and would ask questions. Sometimes, they offered suggestions for areas of personal exploration. One day, I sat down at the computer, started a new journal page, and typed, 'They want me to find joy in grief'. Then I promptly burst into tears. But this concept stuck with me, and I kept asking myself: *Was there joy in grief?*

After days of contemplating, I arrived at an answer. I sat down and asked Joe to be present with me. I told him that his death brought me great sorrow, grief, and sadness. But if I looked deeper, there were also unexpected gifts that came from his death. There were gifts of community, generosity, love, friendship, and family bonds. There were moments of compassion, laughter, and hope. In truth, I couldn't say his death was one thing, for it was many.

Grief is one of the most powerful things I've ever experienced. I will never be as vulnerable, exposed, and searching as I am when I'm grieving. No other emotion would lead me to reach for God in ways I wouldn't have otherwise. I was brought to my knees. I couldn't distract or outrun it. The opposite of love? Indifference. If I do not care about you, I will not grieve you. In some ways, I found that even sadder than grief. My guides told me there are no right or wrong choices in grief. I could lie on the ground in a fetal position, and they loved and supported that decision. I could find my faith and they loved and supported that decision. When I asked why that would be, they responded, 'all paths lead back to God'.

I was supported by most people during this period; however, I could tell there were occasional judgements about how little I publicly showed my emotions. I'd get comments like, 'oh, it hasn't hit you yet', which I found frustrating. Or I'd run into an acquaintance who'd ask, 'How are you?', then stare intently at my face. As an introvert, I found this uncomfortable. I would rattle off a vague reply and then make a quick escape. In looking back, I wonder why I didn't allow others to see my pain. I know most were only offering to walk next to me for a little while. However, I worried that if I didn't hold myself together tightly, I'd unravel at the seams.

For those first months, I remained in a bubble. My memory was significantly affected, and I'd find myself repeating things. This especially irritated Jules, who was asking to be heard. It would take all my energy to focus on a task, like cleaning the kitchen. If I tried to have a conversation while cleaning, I would listen to her answer, only to forget it thirty seconds later. I was constantly saying, 'I'm sorry, I know you just told me, but can you answer that again?'. Or I'd ask about her day, and she'd blow up, 'I JUST told you how it was!'

I also found myself short tempered. After my morning meditation, I felt balanced only to be irritable by the afternoon. Things that would have usually rolled off my back suddenly seemed monumental. There were times when I handled things with grace, and times I'd cringe when a remark would fly from my mouth. This was especially true with the kids. At night, I often laid awake and listed all the ways I was failing as a parent, before vowing to do better the next day.

"Jenny said on the bus that Daddy went to hell because he killed himself," Jules announced, one day after school.

"What?" I asked, caught completely off guard. I knew Jenny's family was religious, but I was shocked someone would say that to Jules directly. I quickly determined that she must have repeated something her parents had said at home.

"Did he go to hell?" Jules asked, looking at me expectantly.

"What do you think?" I asked, allowing myself a moment to collect my thoughts.

She paused, and said reflectively, "It doesn't seem like something God would do."

I nodded in agreement and thought this was a perfect answer. I could tell she was at peace with the conversation, but I wasn't. Inside, I was fuming that someone would say that to her. I wanted to pound on Jenny's front door and yell at her parents: 'How dare you say something that might be repeated to an eight-year-old just months after she lost her father?! If anyone should go to hell- *you* should'.

I had no intention of seeing Jenny's family, but their daughter had a scheduled sleepover at our house the following week. I tried to get Jules to cancel, but she insisted on seeing her friend. When Jenny's father picked her up on Saturday morning, he strolled into my kitchen and commented on a sign with a quote from the bible about faith.

"Faith is really important," he said, with a condescending nod of approval.

"Yes, I believe it is," I replied, trying to sound neutral. I turned and walked to the stairs, while trying to bite my tongue. "Jules, hurry up and get Jenny's things," I yelled, to end the conversation as quickly as possible.

I continued to have frequent reiki sessions with different practitioners. At the time, I might have said that it was out of concern for my heart chakra. But in truth, I deeply wanted to connect with Joe. At every session, I'd pray he would come forward with a message. I wanted him to say something that would heal what was broken inside of me. But I quickly discovered there was a problem: every practitioner read Joe's energy differently. I heard a wide range of descriptions: some told me Joe went to the Light while others said he was an earthbound spirit; some said he was at peace and others said he was unhappy. I often left the sessions feeling more confused than when I'd arrived. The fact that they didn't see Joe the way I did, bothered me.

Seeking answers, I scheduled another intuitive session with the medium, Sara. As the session approached, I was eager to receive some direction. I felt comfortable confiding my frustration regarding other energy workers.

"But why don't they see Joe the same way that I do?" I complained to her during our session.

"Gina," she said, kindly. "Who knew Joe best? You or these people?"

"Well, I did." I said, slowly.

"Exactly! You would know better than any of them. Don't listen to them - what does *your* heart say?" she asked, then waited for a response.

"My heart says he's at peace. Like when I saw him in the session with Lori, he was so happy." I could still picture exactly how he appeared that day.

"Exactly," Sara confirmed. "Remember, it isn't that they are wrong, it's just that they are going to read him differently depending on their own vibration. But he was closest to you, so you go with what *you're* feeling not with what they're feeling."

Her response resonated with me. As we neared the end of the session, I asked her if my Guides had any information regarding my future.

"I think you're in a different job," she said. "I see you at a computer and working with online marketing. You use your creative side, which you enjoy it. You're playing with fonts and colors. Does that make sense to you?"

"Sure," I laughed. "That sounds fun, but I have no background in marketing. Who would possibly hire me for that?"

She paused for a moment before responding. "It's someone that knows you," she said. "I think it starts part-time, but then grows."

That evening, I sat down for a game night with the kids, but my mind was still full of questions. After Joe's death, the kids and I had continued our weekly game of *Sorry*. Jonah volunteered to play Joe's turn and would carefully pick cards and move the green pieces around the board.

"Dad just knocked you out, Mom! SORRY!" Jonah would yell, gleefully, before sending my yellow game piece flying across the board.

"How do you know he'd knock me out?" I'd tease him. "Maybe he'd take out Jules. Look at how many players she has close to home!"

Jonah eyed the board, then shook his head solemnly, "Dad never knocks out Jules, not unless he has to."

"Yeah," Jules chimed in, "Daddy never sends me home, only you and Jonah do!"

"Ok, you're right," I laughed, and pretended to sulk for a minute. "Send my player back home."

There was something comforting in the familiarity of the game. Since we'd often played Joe's turn without him (when he left for AA meetings) it didn't feel strange. In fact, it almost felt like he was with us on those evenings. For a short time, we could almost pretend he was going to walk in the door with a smile, and ask us who had won.

Chapter 13

When the Christmas season arrived, it was an odd place for me to be. I recognized that Joe and I were separated, so Christmas would have looked different anyway, but we'd definitely have spent Christmas Eve together with the kids. In the past, we wrapped presents after the kids went to bed. That year, I went overboard decorating the house for the season to make things feel festive. The porch held bright red banners that read 'Merry and Bright' on the sides of the front door. My brother helped me hang white Christmas lights and we placed a small tree outside, along with a metal sign that said, 'Joy'. I decided to have Joe's extended family over for an open house in mid-December. I thought it would do them good to see the kids. I made a large pot of chili, and the house was soon full of conversations and laughter. Joe's family showered the kids with presents and there were piles of wrapping paper in every corner of the living room. Jules was all smiles as she proudly showed me new LOL dolls and other gifts.

Joe's mom was noticeably absent when the family first walked inside. I realized she was sitting outside, in the car by herself, but I didn't ask questions. I knew coming into the house might be difficult for her. After twenty minutes, I found her standing alone in my front room. She was looking at the pictures on the wall when she caught me watching her.

"I thought it was going to bother me coming in," she said, with tears in her eyes. "But this is your house now and it doesn't feel like him. It feels like you and the kids and that's OK."

Although Joe's picture was in nearly every room of the house, I understood what she meant. It had been over a year since Joe had lived with us and it felt different.

"I guess that's true," I said. I looked around briefly, seeing the house through her eyes before turning my attention back to her. "Why don't you come get something to eat?" I placed a hand gently on her arm to steer her back towards the rest of the family in the kitchen.

As the evening wrapped up, Joe's sister stopped me in the front doorway as we were saying goodbye.

"Do you mind if my kids take a quick look upstairs? They want to see their old rooms." Her request caught me by surprise. We had been in the house for nearly a decade, and I'd forgotten that her kids had grown up there.

"Of course, just ignore the mess," I replied. As they galloped up the stairs like teenagers, I grinned and tried to picture what the house was like when they lived there.

The get-together lifted the kids' spirits, but I knew the holiday was going to be difficult. The year before, I'd given my sister a book called, *The 12 Gifts of Christmas*. Ironically, it was about a woman who lost her husband and she didn't want to celebrate Christmas in her grief. Her children began to anonymously receive Secret Santa presents such as cookies and Christmas decorations. The unexpected gifts helped her family heal. For some reason, the story came to my mind, and I asked my friends if they might consider doing something similar for Jonah and Jules. I worried how the first holiday without their dad might affect them. This amazing group of women didn't have to be asked twice. Shortly before Christmas, mysterious packages began to show up on the front porch. Every day, small items would appear such as candy or lip gloss for Jules (and there were even a few gifts for me). Just like in the book, my kids wanted to know the identity of the 'Ninja Elf'.

"Do you see him?" Jules would yell to Jonah as she squinted into the darkness.

"I'll try upstairs," he'd call, as he raced to look out the front windows.

Every day, they held discussions over the mysterious elf's identity. It was a helpful distraction for them, yet I still grew anxious in the days leading up to Christmas Eve. I kept asking myself how I'd be able to wrap presents and celebrate the holiday alone. My parents decided they'd continue our tradition and host Christmas Eve at their house. I called my dad tearfully one afternoon in December with an unusual request. When Joe passed away, his car was moved from his apartment and placed at my parent's house.

"I need you do something," I said, trying to hold my voice steady. "Can you put a cover over Joe's car, so I don't have to see it in the driveway? I just don't think I can see it right now. It's..." I paused, as a lump formed in my throat.

"Of course," my dad replied, his voice suddenly thick with emotion. "I'll take care of it."

On Christmas Eve, I picked up Chinese takeout and we drove to my parents' house. I was grateful to have some-where to go and the kids were impatient to see their cousins.

We said a prayer before dinner and acknowledged our family in spirit. It seemed strange that Joe was now included in that group. The kids played games well into the evening before we packed up the car to drive home. We listened to Christmas carols and pointed out Christmas lights glowing along the dark country road.

Once home, I put the kids to bed before settling on the couch in my favorite flannel pajamas. A few years before, I had started my own tradition of watching the holiday movie, The Family Stone, on Christmas Eve. That night, I struggled to focus on the movie as I wrapped presents. I couldn't get into the characters, and I was distracted. Certainly, Joe was going to leave me a sign since it was my first holiday without him, and I didn't want to miss it. I waited expectantly for the lights to blink or a lamp to fall. I even secretly hoped he might appear sitting across from me on the couch. I wanted something tangible to know he was with me, but nothing happened. Disappointed, I laid the wrapped presents under the tree, while feeling sorry for myself. I kept glancing around the living room trying to will something to appear. The movie credits began to play, and the house grew still. I sat, feeling empty, as I stared sadly at the Christmas tree. The twinkling lights were blurry through my tears. After several minutes, I stood to go upstairs but then returned to my seat on the couch. *I'll give him a few more minutes,* I thought to myself. *Maybe he just needs more time...* Yet nothing happened. Finally, I went to bed, forlorn, and feeling very alone.

The next day, my brother arrived in the afternoon to put together a new dollhouse from Santa. We sat at the dining room table, listening to 80's music, as we struggled to put the house together.

"This shouldn't be so hard," he laughed, as he tried to force the plastic elevator into place. "I didn't realize I'd need my tool belt and drill."

"Seriously," I said, looking up from placing colored stickers on the dollhouse walls. "Shouldn't the elves do more than leave a box?" I raised my eyebrows.

"How are you guys doing?" he asked, quietly, keeping his eyes on the dollhouse.

"It's hard but we're OK," I shrugged. I wanted to say more, but I didn't know how to put into words my disappointment from the night before. So instead, I busied myself with the stickers.

Jules sprinted into the room with her eyes sparkling. "Is it done yet, Uncle Jason?" She had an armful of small dolls ready to be placed inside.

"Almost, just a few more minutes. Maybe you could get me some more chips," Jason said, as he smiled at her. In that moment I was grateful for his presence; it made the day feel a little less lonely.

"Why wouldn't he have been with me on Christmas?" I demanded to my guides a few days later, after stewing about it. "Why didn't he leave me a sign?"

"Was he not with you?" they asked me. "Or was he just not with you in the way that you expected? Did you really need him in that moment?"

I, stubbornly, had to admit that I didn't actually *need* him physically there. I had the presents wrapped and I could set them out on my own, but I *wanted* him there, just the same. They reminded me that Joe was already with me in all ways that mattered. They said I was never truly alone, even when my mind told me otherwise. I can't say I was satisfied with this answer.

A few nights later, I dreamed that I was in a pet store with Jules, who was looking at puppies (in real life, she'd been asking for a second dog). I was standing in the aisle when Joe suddenly walked into the pet store. I could see him in precise detail: he wore his favorite work blazer, blue jeans, and glasses. I looked at him in surprise and said, "'You aren't supposed to be here'" Somewhere in my mind, I knew he was gone. He smiled at me and replied, "'Of course I'm here. It's an important decision and I want to be a part of it'." When I woke up, I wondered if it had been a visitation dream.

When New Years Eve arrived, it was an odd place to be. As usual, the kids moved forward with more grace. They happily stayed up past their bedtimes with bowls of candy and popcorn. At midnight, we rang in the new year with smiles and hugs. Jules took a black and white picture of the three of us and wrote: *New Years Eve 2018* with a heart around it. As we got ready for bed that night, it felt strange to think about the upcoming year- 2019 – being the first year I would begin without Joe by my side. I began to wonder what I wanted the next year to look like. As I climbed into bed, I was struck by a new emotion. For a moment, I couldn't even name it; then I realized with surprise, that what I was feeling was hope. *I saw that* I had the power to shape the time ahead of me. After months of chaos, the thought was deeply comforting. I turned off the light with a small smile to myself.

Jules and I called out to Joe in the dark, "Happy New Year, good night. We love you!"

As I drifted off to sleep that night, I had a lucid dream. I stood at the wheel of a large wooden ship at sea. I gazed out at the blue horizon with the large white sails billowing behind me. The sky was expansive, and the horizon seemed to stretch forever. There were no boundaries or limits. The next morning, the image was still with me, and the message was clear: *I was the captain of my ship, and I could navigate where I wanted to go. I was the author of my life.* I felt optimistic at the prospect of a different path, but I was also scared. I didn't really know *what* I wanted in life. Although it seemed like a simple question, I couldn't readily find an answer. I began to re-read my journals and saw how often I was afraid of taking risks and played small as a consequence. I resolved to begin to play big and do the things that scared me. I made lists for what I wanted in love, work, and spiritual connection. I reviewed them regularly and focused on seeing the completion of the end goal. In my mind I had visions of cliff diving, writing a book, traveling, falling in love, and having adventures. I set the intention I would have laughter, love, and peace. I asked God to help co-create the best version of my life.

I also began to meditate on a regular basis. Meditation allowed space for me to sit in my heart center. Once I was quiet, I would give God the burdens of what weighed on me. One of my favorite guided meditations involved handing stones over to Jesus. In my imagination, some were small stones that fit in the palm of my hand, while others were heavy, solid boulders. Each day, I was honest in my inventory of what was bothering me. Once I cleared what weighed on my heart, I turned my attention to the future. I would fill my heart with gratitude and set intentions. Some things (like joy) felt out of reach, so I focused on more achievable goals. I touched in with the emotions that I could be present with, such as laughter or happiness. I thought about the things I appreciated, such as coffee with a friend or something funny the kids did that made me laugh. I would hold onto that feeling and think, *I want more of this.* I knew where

I wanted to steer my ship and I held my gaze steady on that horizon.

Once I began to look forward, I also began to make changes for my physical body. Up until that point, I was getting by with processed food, several cups of coffee, cans of soda, and eating bowlfuls of chocolate chips (or anything else put in front of me). I confessed to my counselor how guilty I felt about my food choices and lack of exercise. She reminded me that I was recovering from a trauma and could lower the bar, but I realized that my body truly didn't feel well. I decided to incorporate more fruits and vegetables as a starting point. I read in a book that blueberries are called the 'resurrection fruit'. That resonated, so I put a large bowl of blueberries on my counter. Instead of reaching for chocolate chips, I began polishing off pints of blueberries every day. I focused on making myself healthy meals and slowly began to feel better physically.

One day, my guides told me that my field was clear enough for Joe to come forward if I chose. My stomach flipped at the opportunity of communicating directly with him. I quieted my mind and allowed his words to come forward. He reminded me how much he loved me and the kids. He said that others were deeply grieving his death. He advised me to be kind but cautioned that I shouldn't take on their grief. It was only a few sentences, but I felt a deep sense of peace. When we finished, I asked my guides to give Joe the *biggest* hug in spirit. A loud 'bang, bang, bang', immediately echoed in the empty room. I jumped at the noise and looked around, but nothing had fallen. I realized they honored my request and laughed out loud. A warm sensation blossomed in my heart, and I realized it was starting to mend.

Chapter 14

The plaque for Joe's grave could not be placed over winter due to the frozen ground. As the weather grew warmer, I anticipated the phone call from the cemetery, but it didn't come. It still bothered me that Joe was in an unmarked grave, and I couldn't bring myself to go the cemetery. I checked in with the cemetery, but the staff said the weather had been uncooperative and suggested I call back further into spring.

In April, I was scheduled to take the kids to Universal Studios in Florida. Jason was bringing his daughter, and we had been looking forward to getting away. Yet as the trip neared, I grew anxious about the cemetery plaque. I wanted to have it placed before we left on vacation, but the day before we were due to leave, there was still no word from the cemetery. That morning, I broke down crying and asked Joe to help.

"I know it's not rational," I said, tearfully. "But I can't go on this trip with a light heart knowing that I'm coming home to face the cemetery."

I tried to keep myself busy with last minute errands, but I kept a close eye on my phone, anticipating a call. In the afternoon, I caved and called the cemetery to ask about his plaque.

"Well, it's been raining the last several days and the ground has been really wet," a woman in the office said. I could tell she trying to find the right words to let me down. "It's very doubtful they've been able to complete it but let me check for you." As she placed me on hold, I knew she was going through the motions to appease me, and I felt a pang of disappointment. A few minutes later she came back on the phone.

"Well, this is strange," she said, sounding surprised. "It looks like it was just done this morning. Huh. I can't believe it, that is so strange." She appeared to be searching for an explanation.

"Thank you for checking, I had a feeling," I said quickly, without thinking. I hung up and immediately grabbed my car keys and headed out the front door.

I grew nervous as my car approached the cemetery. I carefully followed the directions I'd written down to find the gravesite, but I surprised myself by recognizing the tree where Joe was buried. I carefully pulled the car to the side of the road. The cemetery grounds were empty except for a few workers in the distance. I walked up the hill as the wind whipped my hair around my face. It was hard to believe that it had been almost eight months since the funeral. As I approached the gravesite, I saw the new bronze plaque had been placed at the foot of the tree. I didn't even see it clearly before I fell to my knees, sobbing. I held my head in my hands and succumbed to the wave of grief.

Once I stopped crying, I examined the plaque more closely. I couldn't stop looking at Joe's name - as if by staring at it, I could force it to make sense. I wasn't supposed to be reading a funeral marker at age forty-three, but maybe that's how it always feels. After a few minutes, I wiped my nose on my jacket, realizing I didn't have any tissues. I took a few deep breaths and asked Joe to send me a sign. Just as I finished the thought, a small black spider fell from the tree limb above and landed squarely on my nose. I jumped back and brushed my face.

"Not quite the sign I was asking for, Joe," I said, with a small laugh. It felt good to smile. I remembered spiders were considered a sign for writing and wondered if he was nudging me to write.

Once I was at the cemetery, I became reluctant to leave; it felt like I was leaving him. I sat in silence for a while then realized I had to meet the school bus so I dragged myself to my feet and made my way back to the car. I cried the whole way home. Later that evening, I sat at the computer and typed a journal entry about the day. I felt Joe say, 'I'm always with you', but I couldn't grasp the message clearly through the fog of grief. But in my mind's eye, I keep seeing him take my shoulders and gently turn me around, as if to say, 'Move forward, Gina'.

We left the following day for Orlando, Florida. It was my first time traveling with the kids without Joe and I was grateful Jason and my niece were with us. Eight-year-old Jules, had a pink cheetah print suitcase packed days in advance. I wanted the trip to Universal Studios to be a happy memory for the kids and I relaxed my normal rules. They were delighted to have towering ice cream sundaes, cotton candy, and late bed-times. Together, we rode the rides at Universal and spent afternoons swimming at the pool.

Joe remained very much on my mind during the trip, but he sent signs that he was with us. I ordered a blanket from room service and was greeted by a man who boomed, "Hello, Ra-HENA," which is exactly how Joe used to say my name jokingly with a fake accent. The staff member must've wondered why I had a stunned look on my face as I accepted the blankets.

On the day in the amusement park, we stood by a stone wall sipping cold drinks. Jonah jumped up from the ground and accidentally struck his head on an overhanging rock. He looked dazed for a moment before touching his head; his hand was coated with blood.

"Mom?" he said, in a frightened tone.

His hair turned dark and matted with blood. People gave us curious stares as we rushed to find the closest first aid station. At the medical station, we were checked in and taken to the examination room.

The medical staff cleaned Jonah's scalp then looked at me and said, "Ok, it's clean. Do you think he needs staples?"

I was surprised at the question since I had no medical background. "I don't know. What are we looking at? Does he need staples?" I asked, anxiously, peering at Jonah's scalp as if the answer would appear on a ten-year-old's head.

"Well, he has about an inch wound on the top of his head. You could take him to the local hospital where they can give him staples."

"Does he need to go?" I asked.

"It's really your decision," he replied.

"What would you do?" I asked.

"It's really your decision," he said again.

"Well, what you would do if it was your child? I'm asking for your opinion," I responded, feeling frustrated at the lack of direction.

He thought for a minute. "I would put ointment and bandage it. If it doesn't reopen, then there's no need to go to the hospital. Just don't swim or go on roller coasters."

With Jonah's head bandaged, we decided to get lunch at the Hard Rock Café. As we approached the restaurant, I thought about how much I missed Joe. *You should be here with me,* I thought. *I can't do this alone.* I was still worried Jonah would need to go to the hospital. We were seated in a booth by a large TV and ordered food. As we ate, I tried to focus on the conversation, but I was distracted. Suddenly, I heard a familiar song and stopped mid-bite to look up at the TV. A video had come on for the song, Tangled Up in Blue, by The Grateful Dead. It wasn't a well-known song, but it was sentimental because Joe used to say it reminded him of me. I realized Joe was letting me know I wasn't alone.

Even with the signs of support, spring was a difficult time for me. The previous months had been a whirlwind of activity. I held my breath while we navigated the will, estate, and guardianships. Now, the estate was closing, and it felt like a chapter was ending. The paralegal dropped off the final paperwork at my home. As I stood in my dining room, a lump formed in my throat. Throughout the estate process, I rarely shed a tear in front of the professionals. I always worried if I started crying, I'd lose control. At each meeting, I'd hold back tears until I was safely back in my car. So on this occasion, my emotions getting the better of me, she looked at me, surprised.

"You'll be ok," she said, giving me a hug.

My guides reminded me that I wasn't leaving Joe behind and yet, it often felt like I was. In my mind, I kept seeing life like a video game. One player exits and continues to watch with interest even though they aren't playing anymore.

In my situation, I stopped to turn and look for Joe rather than continue to play. My guides asked me to pick up the controller and get back into the game of life. They showed the image of Joe standing next to me in spirit, cheering my next move, but I struggled with survivor's guilt.

With other types of death, we hear statements like 'it was just their time' or 'God was ready to call them home'. I didn't have that comfort as a suicide survivor. I could tell my kids, 'Your Dad's mind wasn't thinking clearly from depression. Healthy, he would've never done this', but I couldn't change his final act. At times, the selfishness of it felt like being kicked while I was down. It made moving forward difficult. I knew in spirit Joe was loving and supportive because he always told me how proud he was of me and how much he loved us. But remembering his personality towards the end of his life made it complicated. I often had a hard time reconciling the two versions. *Am I really getting messages from Joe or is this just my subconscious telling me what I want to hear?* I wanted absolutes – yet nothing is absolute in grief.

One day I was sitting in morning traffic when the song, Don't Cry by Guns N' Roses, came up on the radio. For some reason, the song reminded me of the night I found out Joe had died, when someone sat on the bed with me. *Was that Joe?* I had wondered about this more than once. I thought about what he would have wanted to say in that moment. It was strange, but the lyrics of the song seemed to fit by offering words of comfort to the person being left behind. In that moment, I strongly felt Joe and my heart filled with love for him. 'I love you so much," I said silently to him. I returned my eyes to the road as traffic started to move and I blinked in surprise. Through my tears, I read the license plate on the car directly in front of me. It contained the most beautiful message I could've received, it simply read: **LVUMORE.**

Despite the signs, I struggled to reach some form of acceptance. Joe came forward and told me I carried a false sense of responsibility for his actions. He reminded me I wasn't responsible, and his actions were his alone. In counseling sessions, I began to explore the co-dependent nature of our marriage. I had heard the term co-dependent previously in Al Anon, but I disliked the term because it felt like a criticism of our relationship. Joe and I may have been co-dependent, but we didn't love each other any less because of it. Sometimes I felt co-dependent love was more complex for we read each other's subtle cues and responded; if he was up, I was down and vice versa. It took a deep level of connection to maintain balance. But as I explored co-dependency, I also saw how often I tried to control Joe. I wanted to control his alcoholism, dictate his sobriety, and make decisions for him. Although it stemmed from a desire to make things better, I began to consider what message this sent him over the years. Even after he died, I still wanted to override his opinion and change his last days. I had never stopped to think about his perspective.

Years ago, I read a book that stated people who commit suicide often did so because of a life plan. The author said that prior to an incarnation, the souls involved would agree to the plan. There would be specific lessons for the person that committed suicide as well as family and friends left behind. It was a concept that both frightened and intrigued me. Yet a memory had re-surfaced a few weeks after Joe died and remained with me.

When I was in my late twenties my best friend, Kristin, invited me to a potluck. At the time, I was married to my first husband and happy for a reason to leave the house. I found myself in a small kitchen with mostly strangers. Part of the group started talking about psychics and someone eagerly said that a psychic was attending. Apparently, the woman was employed as a cab driver during the day but loved to give impromptu readings. I anticipated her arrival but was surprised when she finally walked in the door; she was short with dirty hair, disheveled clothes, and several missing teeth. However, I was curious, so I readily agreed for a reading. She took my hand and told me that my marriage would soon end with a divorce, and I felt relieved. She predicted in a few years; I would marry my soul mate and we would have two children. She noted it was undetermined if we would choose to have the third child but if we did, a soul was ready to step into that role. She predicted my second husband would die in his early forties but didn't give a cause. She went on to say more, but I tuned out because the rest seemed like a lifetime away.

A few years later, when Joe and I got back together, her prediction bothered me, so I buried the memory. Time went by until I completely forgot about it. But a few weeks after Joe died, the memory hit me out of the blue. *Oh my God, someone actually predicted this,* I thought. I frantically tried to recall the rest of the reading, but it was blank. I realized she had been eerily accurate both in Joe's death and about the possibility of a third child. It was something we had discussed extensively when the kids were in preschool but opted not to pursue.

Was this Joe's life plan? I started to ask myself. I found myself asking big, unanswerable questions like, *What if he wanted to experience suicide? What if he knew this was how his life would end and agreed to it?* Questioning my inner dialogue was difficult but it helped me detach from feelings of guilt.

When I found myself trying to re-write Joe's life, I reminded myself it was not my story. Sometimes I even visualized handing a pencil back to Joe (and God). It became a practice I revisited often, yet the concept of a life plan was difficult for me to accept. Joe said more than once that he simply reached the end of the road. I acknowledged that my real desire was to bring him back 100% healthy. If I merely had the power to bring him back to the depression he suffered at the end, I couldn't do it. *How could I wish someone I loved to be in that much pain?*

Chapter 15

When Joe died, a friend gave me literature from a local program called LOSS, which focused on support for suicide survivors. That spring, they held a bowling fundraiser for their survivor outreach program. I thought it would be a good way to honor Joe's memory and so I organized Team Kitzmiller to bowl with some friends and family. I purchased blue football jerseys for the kids and myself to wear to the event. We each chose a number and nickname for the jersey and had Team Kitzmiller printed on the back. I chose number 10 (for Joe's birthday) and the name Reggie (the nickname Joe used for me).

That morning, something unexpected happened. I sat in meditation and filled my heart with love. I felt Joe come forward with a message, but then I did something different; I picked up a pen and started writing the message in my notebook. To my surprise, a letter from Joe emerged. In it, he told me he was always with me and the kids. He said he was watching life through our eyes, and he didn't feel separate. He loved the T-shirts and thanked me for honoring him with the event. When I was done, I sat back in quiet contemplation.

Afterwards, re-reading the note multiple times, I asked myself if it was real. My logical mind questioned it, but something felt authentic to me. I tucked the notebook away but returned to look at it often over the next several weeks.

During the LOSS bowling fundraiser, they showed Joe's picture in a video presentation honoring those who passed from suicide. His picture still looked out of place to me. My mind still couldn't accept him as part of that group. I was briefly uncomfortable and deliberately turned my attention back to family and friends. It was a large gathering, so it wasn't hard to become distracted. Jonah stayed by the bowling lane and focused on getting a high score while Jules was fixated on the silent auction. She had never seen one and dragged me around to bid on multiple items. We walked out with an armful of things that she 'won', and she was pleased with herself. That evening, the kids settled inside to watch TV, tired from the event. My dad and I stood in the driveway while I eyed down my nemesis, the lawnmower.

"Are you sure I can do this?" I asked my dad for the tenth time.

"It's not hard, Gina," he said. "You remove the gas cap and fill it to about this line." He pointed to a small green line in the tank then screwed the cap back into place. "Then replace the cap and pull the string to start the mower. I'll help change the oil when it's needed. There's a sticker right here if you forget what to do and you have the manual."

I still looked at the mower suspiciously. I'd never pushed a mower before because Joe had handled all of the yardwork. Since his death, I had a new appreciation for how much time he put into it. It was something I'd taken for granted. Throughout the fall, friends and my neighbor generously mowed the yard. But it was now spring in Ohio and the mowing season was upon us. My neighbor had offered to continue to mow but now that winter was over, it was time for me to learn how to do it for myself. It was just one of the many steps towards being more independent. *Ok. I've got this*, I thought to myself.

"You know, it's your fault I'm paranoid about this," I said, in a teasing tone to my dad. "Do you remember when we were little? You let me try the riding mower *one* time because Mom said we needed 'gender equality'. Jason had to wash dishes and I got to mow the yard. But I did such a bad job, you switched us back and gender equality was never mentioned in our house again."

My dad chuckled. "I do kind of remember that. You left tufts of grass everywhere and we had to re-mow," he smiled. "Well, this will be easier- just follow a straight line."

He pulled the cord, and the motor came to life with a loud roar. I looked around at my neighbors' houses, suddenly self-conscious. What other forty-three-year-old woman was getting a mowing lesson from her *dad*? I was glad it was evening because I hoped no one would notice me. I looked up just as some neighbors walked by with their dog. I gave a little wave and tried not to appear as embarrassed as I felt. My dad showed me how to lower the blade and then he walked the mower across the yard under my watchful eye.

"Hey, this has some power. Watch this!" He increased the speed and began to pretend like he was jogging behind it. Despite my self-consciousness, I laughed at how ridiculous he looked.

"Oh my God, Dad. My neighbors must think we're insane," I said, as I giggled. "But I guess it is a Honda mower. Alright, let me try." I turned the mower around and mowed a straight line across my front yard. Not to be outdone, I pretended like I was running towards him with high knees, and he started laughing.

"Who knew learning to mow would be so fun? Joe would've gotten a kick out of this," I said. "He's probably laughing at us right now."

"Yeah, I think so," said my dad, smiling. "Do you need me to come back over tomorrow to help?"

I said a quick prayer of gratitude for him. I'd been dreading learning how to mow but the lesson had turned out to be enjoyable.

"No, I think I've got it, you can just be my emergency backup," I joked. I realized I was feeling confident about trying it on my own. *Joe- are you seeing this?* I thought, as we walked the mower back to the garage. *Me? Mowing? Who knew it would feel so momentous- I hope you got a good laugh!*

Over the next few months, I began updating the house. I painted my bedroom walls from dark blue to a bright yellow. I purchased new carpet and furniture for the living rooms. I reorganized closets and even cleaned the basement. Every time I made a room my own, I felt like I was moving forward in grief. The changes in the house helped me see that I was making progress. But sometimes, the urge to change something came from anxiety (like the time I left ground beef cooking on the stove because I had a sudden compulsion to touch up paint in the hallway). I worried that Joe might be upset with the changes because we rarely agreed on updates for the house. I tiptoed around the issue and didn't talk to him as much for a few days. I felt a sense of relief when he came forward and told me that he saw the changes and wasn't upset. He said he understood this was my way of moving forward.

One of the last purchases was an oversized bean bag for the living room. I wanted something comfy for the kids to lounge on while watching TV or playing video games. Jules was excited when she saw an enormous box on the front porch. Jonah and I struggled to maneuver it into the living room and pull out the giant bean bag. As we cut away the plastic wrap and unwrapped the bag, we noticed a large tag attached to the side. In white block letters, it read, 'Big Joe'. Jonah and Jules looked up at me in surprise, it was so close to their nickname for their dad, 'Big Daddy Joe'.

"Mom, do you see the tag?" Jonah asked. "Did you know it was on here?" he asked, with a curious look, but I was speechless.

"I had no idea, it's from Amazon," I said, stumped. I couldn't recall the name of the company that made the beanbag. "I guess your dad's letting us know he's with us."

The kids were a bit awestruck, and they asked me all sorts of questions about how it came to be. I couldn't quite explain it, but the physical reminder of Joe's support made me smile every time I walked into the living room and saw it.

Even with signs of Joe's support, I found myself lonely at times. I realized that I wanted to have love in my life again; I wanted to have a family and to be part of a couple. And I wanted that space to be filled with the right person for me and for my kids. My guides told me that if I wanted to call in love, I needed to raise my vibration to meet it. I took their advice and began to visualize the ideal relationship. I wrote down the qualities I wanted in a life partner. It sounds strange, but I felt gratitude for this person, that I'd never met. Some days I wondered if they were having a bad day or difficult life events.

I also began to project my gratitude for future events. I imagined myself at my 20th wedding anniversary. I pictured what I was wearing, who was sitting around me, and the emotions of the moment. I put aside my rational mind and focused on every detail I could imagine. I pictured a group sitting at a long table that included my spouse, my children (grown and with partners), adult stepchildren, and grandchildren running around the room. I pictured my husband's hand in mine and how it would feel to rest my head on his shoulder. I felt the joy of looking at our family. I also pictured my husband giving a toast and what he would say in it. The first time I did the meditation, I felt it so clearly that it brought tears to my eyes. But I didn't always see the end goal so vividly. There were times when I sat down to meditate and the visual felt forced or I couldn't tap into the emotion of it. Sometimes the meditation brought up mixed emotions for me. I knew what was in my heart, but I also felt conflicted. I worried that Joe would be offended by my desire for a new relationship. I pictured him saying, 'Well, it didn't take her long to move on'. But as always, Joe remained supportive. He said he understood that I wasn't replacing him and encouraged me to open my heart.

About seven months after Joe's death, I decided it was time to start dating again. I joined an online dating site and went on my first date. I was nervous and worried we wouldn't have anything to talk about. However, it exceeded my expectations. The man was easy to talk to and I found myself laughing more than I had in months. For a moment, I stepped out of my role of widow, and it felt nice to have a conversation with someone who didn't know my history. When I got home that night and put the kids to bed, I found myself telling stories from the early days of my relationship with Joe. I recalled how he would eat spicy, left-over Mexican food for breakfast with coffee and I thought it was the weirdest thing, until I tried it and loved it. The kids were still giggling as I turned out the lights. Feeling nostalgic, I ended up staying up late and tearfully looking through old pictures and wondering, *how exactly did I get here?*

I continued to go out on dates because I figured that if I asked the universe for love, I should show that I was open to finding it. Although I met some nice men through online dating, it never went beyond a few weeks and, at times, I became frustrated. My guides reminded me that love would happen in God's time, not mine. They also pointed out that I was receiving companionship and wasn't that what I'd asked for? As summer arrived, my intentions for love began to take root. I had no way of knowing the seed had been planted months before, at a time when I least expected it.

The day after the funeral, I had received an email from someone I didn't know, named Matt. He explained that his son was in Jules' school, and he had lost his wife, Samantha, the year before to breast cancer. He'd been on the receiving end of so much generosity that he wanted to pay it forward. He said that if I had questions about grief or about social security to reach out to him. I had a few questions about the social security process and responded with a short email. The thought crossed my mind that maybe he was reaching out for a romantic interest, but it became apparent that wasn't his intent. He detailed his love for his wife with such beauty and sincerity, there was no doubt about his integrity. While reading his email, I thought to myself, *good luck to the next woman this guy dates.* I couldn't imagine someone writing such a poetic description about me.

Over the months, Matt and I emailed each other occasionally. The emails were brief, but I found comfort in knowing there was someone out there who was familiar with the road of grief; someone who got *it* without me having to explain. I could ask him questions that no one else could answer for me. Things like what to expect for first Christmas or when to visit the cemetery with the kids. He always gave well thought out replies. At the time, I wondered if it wasn't helping him with his own grief- being able to reflect a full year later. We finally met in person for the first time at a school event in the spring. It was nice to put a face to the name and to meet his children. I can't say either one of us gave it much more thought.

The first Mother's Day was difficult for me. I took the kids to a restaurant, but it felt odd to be just the three of us. I tried not to let it bother me, but inside I was sad. I looked around at the other families and felt like an outsider. I couldn't help but think of how drastically my life had changed over the course of a few years. That night, I checked my email and found one from Matt. "Hi, Gina! Not sure when you will receive this email, but I want to wish you a happy Mother's Day. This being the first Mother's Day you are celebrating on your own, maybe it will be a hard one for you. I hope you don't feel too alone and that you are able to pull joy from the time you spend with Jonah and Jules. I wish you a wonderful Mother's Day. I am amazed at how much moms do every day (especially now!) and celebrate you today!" It was brief, but his email made me feel a little less lonely. That night in bed, when I reviewed the day, I found myself grateful for his friendship. A short while later, when he told me about an overseas trip he had planned with his two kids, I found myself admiring his confidence. I couldn't imagine crossing the world, handling passports and connections by myself.

In early July, while Matt was away on that trip with his kids, I took Jules and a friend to a local park one day. I took a book with me and planned to sit and read while they played. I spotted a bench across the playground and walked over to it. As I read the inscription, I realized with surprise that it was dedicated to Matt's late wife. I sat down and opened my book, but I struggled to focus on the page. I kept thinking about Matt being so far away and here I was, sitting on his wife's bench. I felt a strange connection to this stranger I barely knew. I suddenly wished I had his phone number so I could text him, 'Hey! I'm sitting on your bench and keeping it warm for you'. I watched Jules swinging back and forth and realized that I wanted to know more about him.

The next week, I was back in the rural town of McConnelsville to meet with Lori for another reiki session. My heart was still longing for companionship, and I asked her when I was going to find love. She said that she felt 'my guy' was close and asked if I had recently met someone.

"Well, no. Not really," I said. Sensing my hesitation, she raised an eyebrow and waited for me to elaborate. "There is this one guy…but I don't know. I don't even know him." I proceeded to explain how I'd come to know Matt and the strange coincidence with the park bench.

"I think that's him! Show me a picture!" she said, excitedly.

I pulled out my phone and scanned social media until I found his profile. I pulled up a picture from his Facebook page.

"That's Matt," I said, feeling silly as I handed her the phone. She enlarged the picture and studied his face.

"That's him!" she grinned, as she handed the phone back to me. "This is the guy, I'm sure of it. You should reach out to him."

"Well, that's funny, because I actually thought that on the drive here. I wanted to ask him to meet for coffee, but I don't know…" my voice trailed off.

"Give it a chance. It starts slow, but you fall in love. It's his kindness that draws you to him," she said, as she handed the phone back to me. I looked down at the picture of a relative stranger and wondered if she was right.

When Matt returned from his trip, I suggested we meet for coffee. I entered the coffee shop and found him waiting inside. He was tall and thin, wearing jeans and t-shirt. I stole a few glances at him as we waited for our order. I didn't know this person at all. *Do I fall in love and marry this man?* I wondered. We sat down at a small table, and he showed me pictures of his trip. It was interesting to see pictures of his children and hear about their travels. At one point, he paused in the middle of a story and his entire face lit up with a smile. My stomach flipped and I began to talk nervously. As I left the coffee shop, I laughed and shook my head, thinking I'd made a horrible first impression. But later that night, I received an email from Matt, asking if we could meet for coffee again the following Friday. A smile spread across my face as I read his message.

The next week, the weather was pleasant and sunny, so we decided to have coffee outside. We drove to a nearby neighborhood and found a park bench that overlooked a shaded pond. The morning passed by as we talked effortlessly with each other. For the rest of the summer into fall, we spent every Friday morning together. We sat on 'our bench' and discussed our lives. We talked openly about Joe and Samantha and candidly shared stories of our loss. Sitting next to Matt, I found myself opening in ways that I rarely did outside my inner circle. Friday quickly became my favorite part of the week.

In August, I visited close friends in St. Petersburg, Florida. As we drove into town from the airport, I pointed out the

Don Cesar to the kids. The towering pink hotel was impossible to miss.

"That's where your dad and I were married," I said.

The kids and I spent the day on the beach and basked in the sunshine. But in the afternoon, a rainstorm rolled in from the gulf and the sky turned dark. It continued to rain into the evening, and we darted into a beach restaurant for dinner with my friends. Our group sat by a window and watched the storm outside while eating seafood. Kelly's husband suggested we still try to see the sunset after dinner. He thought the weather might improve, but I held out little hope. However, as we left the restaurant, the rain began to taper, and the sky lightened. Kelly asked if we'd like to walk out to the beach and the kids agreed. They ran ahead towards the water with the sand still damp from the rain.

Kelly and I were walking down the beach, talking, when I turned to see one of the most beautiful sunsets I have ever witnessed. The gulf sky was breathtaking – it was ablaze in deep orange and pink hues. After gazing at the sight for a few minutes, we turned away from the ocean horizon only to see a rainbow appear overhead. It grew until we could see the entire rainbow from end to end with a second rainbow start to form behind it. Everyone on the beach was wonderstruck; people were pointing, talking excitedly, and taking photos. I kept turning to view the rainbow then back to the sunset in amazement.

Kelly walked up next to me and remarked, "Clearly, this is Joe. Who else would it be?"

Her comment made me smile and I silently sent a 'thank you' before joining the kids for pictures. I stood between Jonah and Jules with my arms around them. At age eleven, Jonah was normally 'too cool' for pictures with his mom, but he rested his head on my shoulder and the camera captured him in a moment of laughter. To this day, it is my favorite picture ever taken of him.

During our trip, Kelly and I were able to spend time alone on her back patio and I found myself telling her about Matt. I knew I enjoyed being with him, but I wasn't sure how he felt about me. She encouraged me to take the next step and let him know I wanted to be more than friends. The next day, she took a picture of me in a beach chair with a margarita in hand. I felt awkward sending Matt a picture of myself in a bikini but I captioned it, 'greetings from St. Pete' and hit the send button. He responded immediately and I felt that we had shifted to something beyond friends. When I returned, Matt and I resumed our Friday morning coffee dates. After a few weeks, Matt suggested we go on an *actual* date and I was excited. We went to dinner at a Japanese restaurant then stopped by a coffee shop for bubble tea. Not wanting the date to end, we ended up driving for a long time on back country roads and I even showed him my childhood home. While we drove, we told each other stories from high school.

"Hey, I saw on Facebook that you know Carrie Miller too. How do you know her?" I asked him.

"Carrie? You know her? I grew up next door to her. My parents still live next door to her parents." Matt responded.

"Seriously? I lived with her for the last month or two of high school. I think my mom was happy to get a break from me." I laughed.

"You actually lived next door to me?" Matt said, incredulously. "I was in college, but I was home all the time. That's so weird! I wonder if I saw you."

It felt like a strange coincidence and one of many we shared. I found out later that Matt's wife passed away from cancer almost a year to the day that Joe died. I also learned that Matt's wedding reception was held at the same location as Joe's first wedding that I had attended. Every time I felt unsure, a coincidence would appear.

The following week, we went to see a movie. Sometime during the movie, Matt took my hand, and I rested my head on his shoulder. The movie credits started to roll, yet suddenly I didn't want to leave. Something was stirring in my heart. We sat for a few minutes watching the rest of the auditorium empty before leaving our seats. As I walked next to Matt, I ducked my head so my hair fell over the side of my face, creating a shield - unsure of how to express what I was feeling.

As summer ended, I struggled with the fact that the first anniversary was approaching. I wasn't sure how to handle dates with the kids. *Do I tell them the actual date Joe died or the date we found out about his death?* I discussed my concerns with their counselor, and she suggested I tell them the actual date of Joe's death and use it moving forward. In her opinion, dates were not important to children and Jules needed to know Joe didn't forget her birthday. Shortly after the session, I sat the kids down and discussed the anniversary dates. I tried to keep it short and to the point. They shrugged and said they didn't have a preference. I was confused by the lack of response. I wondered if I had explained it correctly. *Would the date haunt them the way it haunted me?* On some level, I understood that Joe didn't view his death as tragic. But although I was grateful to know he was at peace; I couldn't let go of the emotion surrounding his death.

In the past, I've told earthbound spirits that tragic events will always *feel* tragic and that by going into the Light, they are not saying what happened to them was OK because some things would never be 'OK'. In my heart, Joe's death would never be 'OK', but I trusted in a bigger picture that I couldn't see. God did not send his death, but He certainly foresaw it. Joe's choices would always remain *his* choices; but I got to choose too; I could choose to stand in faith. On good days, I began to see how our relationship remained much the same. Joe was still on my team; it just wasn't in the way I had imagined.

About a month before the anniversary of Joe's death, a family member on Joe's side of the family committed suicide. Joe's sister texted to request the contact information for the pastor that spoke at Joe's funeral. As I dialed my brother's number for the information, I felt like I'd stepped backwards in time. I hung up the phone and found myself emotionally unraveling. I suddenly wanted Joe's reassurance. I could feel so acutely the space where he should have been. I called him forward and told him how I was feeling about the loss. I acknowledged that it wasn't my loss and yet it had caused feelings of grief to resurface. As I sat with him, I confessed that I was also struggling to parent alone. Jules was contending with drama in her friend group and I found myself annoyed with the young girls' behavior instead of really listening. I remembered how Joe would listen wholeheartedly to a person without giving an opinion. I knew this was what Jules needed, and yet it was difficult for me.

"I'm not like you!" I said to him, tearfully. "You could do this so easily and the kids need you <u>here</u> to balance this with me!" Inside, I knew what I was really saying was, 'I'm not good enough to do this alone'.

I started crying harder, and suddenly the energy shifted in my chest. It felt like someone had reached in and lifted something out of my heart. Surprised, I took a deep breath and realized Joe had removed something to help me. He asked if I could let go of the story that I was alone. As I allowed my emotions to settle, he encouraged me to open my heart more with Matt. I was grateful for his support, but I felt pulled in two different directions. I was at the beginning of a new relationship, while still deeply grieving the one that I'd lost. Anytime I felt happy, a voice in my head would whisper, *'how can you be doing so well?'*. It was eating away at my sense of peace. I knew it was natural to move on to a new relationship, especially since Joe and I had been separated, but I judged myself for it. *Wasn't I confirming what he thought in life; that we could move on without him?* That thought would pull me backward and spiral me into the darkness of shame.

One day, I found myself thinking about Joe as I completed a long run through the neighborhood. My feet fell rhythmically on the sidewalk, and I grew contemplative. I realized that I still hadn't figured out *how* to really let him go. As I continued running, I became frustrated, and angry tears blurred my vision. I heard Joe ask me to let go of my guilt. He kept saying it wasn't mine to carry, but I couldn't do it. 'If we separated and I killed myself, don't tell me you wouldn't be in a fetal position in a corner somewhere!' I said to him angrily in my mind, 'So don't talk to *me* about guilt!' Emotionally, I knew I'd run into a brick wall and yet I couldn't seem to navigate around it.

Every day, I asked God for help with my feelings for Matt. I didn't want to sabotage a healthy relationship because I was still in process with the old one. Frankly, I was deeply angry that I even had to be *in* process; I couldn't understand why I felt so deeply tied to our relationship. In some ways, I was still grieving the loss of our marriage and Joe's death at the same time. *It's been almost two years since we separated – why can't I move past this?* I wondered.

I met with my counselor and for the first time in months, I cried the entire session. I cried for the loss of my marriage, for the guilt I couldn't shake, for the trauma of Joe's death... for all of it. She gave me space to feel the emotions, then reminded me that Joe was the one in control of his life. She pointed out that he made a thousand choices leading up to his death and I did not bear responsibility for those decisions. For the first time, I began to open to the possibility that she was right. Once I was alone, I opened my heart to God and took the time to explore my emotions. I realized at the center was the fear that I'd failed Joe; I should have been more for him. I asked for God's help to see the truth and continued to ponder this for days.

Over time, I saw it was often small thoughts that pulled me out of balance. Like a leaky faucet, drops of negative thinking could become destructive. A small negative thought might be a seed today, but if left undetected, it would grow into a large weed. If I ignored them, the weeds would eventually overtake my garden.

Mistakenly, I thought my love had to be equivalent to how much pain I was willing to bear in grief. It took me a long time to realize that Joe's happiness in spirit didn't change based on how much I was grieving him. *Look how much pain I'm willing to be in to show that I care about you,* was my irrational logic. Slowly, I began to see this wasn't true. I realized that Joe in spirit was completely at peace. I could choose to be miserable, but that didn't make him feel more loved. I saw the way I had wrapped myself in a blanket of grief and thought, *he's gone so I must be gone too.* The realization created a shift in how I processed my feelings. I began to pay close attention to my emotions and the thoughts that preceded them. I saw how my thoughts dictated my emotions. Thoughts like, *he is gone,* or *I'm alone,* made me feel separated. I began replacing them with thoughts that brought me peace, such as, *Joe is still with me.* It didn't shift overnight, but gradually this practice helped me let go of the thoughts that only made me miserable.

One morning in meditation, I called in my team along with Joe and opened my heart for intuitive guidance. I knew there were areas that needed healing in my heart. After sitting silently, I found myself unexpectedly re-visiting the memory from the night I received the phone call about Joe's death. Strangely, I saw the scene as if I was outside of it. 'Gina' was sitting by herself on the couch, crying in the dark living room. I found myself wanting to comfort her so I walked over and sat beside her while Joe sat on the other side. I began to send healing energy to her heart and felt Joe do the same.

"Does she know we're here?" I asked, after a few minutes. I looked past her profile at Joe, who was gazing at her intently.

"No, but she knows someone is here," he said, quietly. He lovingly reached over and brushed an invisible hair from her face. "She can sense something."

We continued to sit for a while before leaving the memory. When I came out of the meditation, I sat peacefully with my thoughts. I remembered the details of that night and a few unexplained pieces fell into place. I recalled feeling someone touch my cheek along with a sensation on my arm. I had read that time wasn't linear, but my mind couldn't make sense of it. *Was that Joe? Were we both there? But how is that possible?* Despite my questions, I couldn't help but feel a sense of wonder.

Around this time, I heard about the Lion's Gate Portal (when the star, Sirius, becomes visible in the sky). I didn't normally pay attention to astrology, but my guides nudged me to use this time to set intentions. At the last minute,

I decided to attend a gathering to honor the portal. I arrived at the event space and settled in a plush chair with a notebook. The leader directed us through a meditation then announced she would privately give each participant a message from those in spirit. My ears perked up and I was curious to see what message I'd receive. When it was my turn, she led me into a separate room that was painted so darkly the walls looked like they were covered in velvet. I looked around the room as the medium closed her eyes and tuned in.

"I see a white crown of roses on your head," she said.

I nodded and waited for her to say more. For the first time, I realized I didn't feel a desperate need to hear from Joe. I'd been communicating with him so frequently that my heart felt content. The medium asked if I was in a relationship and I admitted I was in a new relationship after my husband passed away by suicide. As soon as I mentioned the word suicide, I felt her demeanor change.

"Your husband's energy is still trying to pull you down," she said. "It's an unhealthy relationship. He's unhappy and not learning from his choices. You need to sever the tie to him."

I frowned and eyed her suspiciously. I suspected she wouldn't have given the same answer if I had said Joe passed away from cancer. The entire message rang false, and I found myself irritated as I gathered my things to leave. Driving home, I called my guides forward.

"Why would she read his personality like that?" I complained, out loud. "That's not how I see Joe at all, and we talk all the time. He's been nothing but supportive and he's always encouraging me to open my heart to Matt. I don't get it!"

After voicing my concerns, I set the reading aside. I didn't like the woman's energy and I didn't believe the reading was valid. A few days later, my guides confirmed it was not accurate. They said the first part of the message was correct regarding the crown of white roses to symbolize my growing faith. However, they said the second part was false and suggested I give it no further thought. In some ways, it felt like a redemption because I had honored my intuition. I realized that even if a famous medium gave a message from Joe, I wouldn't accept it as the truth if it didn't resonate with me. I saw that I didn't have to accept someone else's opinion and it felt good to stand in my own power.

I woke up on September 27, 2019, to the realization that it was exactly 365 days since I had last seen Joe alive. I remembered that we had gone to the bank to discuss separating accounts. It was a painful process. The bank manager recalled meeting us and later told me that she remembered Joe gave me a long hug when we finished the paperwork. I have revisited that memory more times than I can count. I wish I'd paid more attention to that hug, but I was distracted. If I could go back, I would soak up every second of it.

As the anniversary approached, I had high expectations. I imagined a day full of fun activities for the kids so they wouldn't have time to be sad. *We are going to be positive and have a good day!* I told myself in the days leading up to the date. But when I woke up on the day itself, the fog of grief had rolled in unexpectedly. I felt weighed down with a heaviness that made moving difficult. I struggled to make breakfast for the kids, and afterwards climbed back into bed, looking for a place to escape. I felt Joe nudge me and suggest I do something with the kids.

"I know, but I can't right now. Just let me be," I mumbled, exhausted. I pulled the cover over my face and fell back to sleep. It was early afternoon before I dragged myself out of bed, feeling groggy. I walked into the living room to find both kids lying quietly on the couches. To my surprise, they weren't on their phones or watching TV and I realized I needed to do something. I showered and suggested we get lunch at Taco Bell (Joe's favorite restaurant). The kids liked the idea and scrambled off the couches to race to the car. I wasn't used to ordering Taco Bell and ordered too much food for the three of us. This brightened their mood; they teased me about my Taco Bell ordering inadequacy and recalled how their dad had it down to a science. After lunch, one of my friends suggested we take the kids to a fall festival in town. The small, community festival had live music, bounce houses, and fair food. I took in the fall sunshine as I watched the kids dart in and out of the bounce houses. Although it didn't erase my sadness, I appreciated being surrounded by close friends.

That night, Jules and I scrolled through Netflix looking for a movie to watch together. We decided on CoCo, which we had seen a few years prior in the theater. I remembered the movie focused on family bonds and how those in spirit remain with us. It turned out to be the perfect choice. When the movie ended, it was just after 10pm. I remembered that a police officer commented that Joe passed around that time (although I can't say for certain that is accurate). I gathered the kids to light a candle for their dad. I asked one of them to read the poem, We Remember Them, because I knew I couldn't repeat the words out loud without breaking down.

"As long as we live, they too will live. For they are now a part of us. As we remember them," Jules solemnly read.

My eyes filled with tears as I watched her. We told Joe we loved him before blowing out the candle and heading to bed. The day had been harder than I had expected.

I climbed into bed, exhausted, and relieved to put the day behind me.

I prepared to celebrate Jules nineth birthday on October 1st. Earlier in the week, Joe asked me to pick out a separate card from him. I laughed because the card I intuitively picked was expensive and covered in glitter. Mentally, I teased him about this because it was unlike him in life. I felt his laughter as he responded that he said he'd help pick the 'perfect card', not the cheapest. I filled out the card with a message from him. It wasn't what I would have said, but I trusted it needed to be his words, not mine. Sure enough, Jules' eyes lit up as she was reading it and she giggled when he said he saw the girl drama going on at school. It was exactly what she needed to hear from her dad.

October continued to mark one-year anniversaries. Joe's birthday was the following week. I drove out of town to meet an old co-worker for lunch. On the way home, I decided I would take the kids to the cemetery to honor Joe's birthday. I was listening to U2, when I felt a nudge from Joe. He said he didn't want me to take the kids to the cemetery. He said it would only make them sad and that wasn't his wish on his birthday. He said he felt strongly about this and advised me against it. I can't say I agreed but I wanted to honor his wishes. I walked in the house with desserts for the kids. I told them it was their dad's birthday but didn't make a big deal about it. That evening, the three of us went outside to throw the football. The weather was perfect as the three of us laughed and ran around the neighborhood court. As I tossed the football and looked at my kids smiling, I realized Joe had been right.

That night, I wrote in my journal, 'I keep thinking about losing someone to suicide. The part where I get stuck is knowing that they killed themselves with the mindset of 'Your lives will be better without me', so it's difficult when life starts to re-balance and happiness comes back. There is always a hole and sadness where you'd like that person to be, but laughter, happiness, and joy do return. I have to keep reminding myself how happy he is and that he's no longer in that place. None of us are in the place we were last year.'

My birthday arrived the following week and as I meditated that morning, I felt deep gratitude for all that I had been given. I reflected on the previous year and saw how God and the universe worked on my behalf. I acknowledged the synchronicities that had brought me to that exact moment, and I felt a deep peace in my heart. I went to a birthday dinner that night with my brother and my friends. I found myself at ease and enjoying the moment with friends and family. As Jason turned into the neighborhood, the opening notes of Don't Stop Believing began to play on the radio. I turned and punched Jason's arm in excitement. "It's Journey! It must be Joe telling us Happy Birthday!" I exclaimed. I couldn't help but smile as I tried to coax him to sing along.

Chapter 16

O n October 20, 2019, I anxiously rubbed my cold hands together in anticipation for the start of the Nation-wide Children's Marathon held in downtown Columbus, Ohio. My mind was filled with questions about what the next 26.2 miles held in store for me. *Would I be able to complete it? Would it be painful?*

I had gotten back on the treadmill during the previous winter. Although I'd not been actively running, slowly the thought had formed, *I should run the full marathon in October.* I knew it would be symbolic to mark the first anniversary. I also wanted to show the kids (and myself) that I could move forward in grief, and that it was ok to have new experiences. In my adrenaline rush, I signed up online and posted about it on social media. The next day, I panicked and wondered what I'd done. I hadn't been consistently running and was now forty-three years old. I knew my decision was met with some skepticism for I'd virtually no training under my belt, but I pushed my fears aside. I knew I needed to run the marathon. I researched programs online and found a run-walk program by Jeff Galloway that seemed reasonable and started training.

The training runs during the winter were beneficial for me. I was never someone who ran during cold weather, and I took pride in layering up and heading out in frigid temperatures. It turns out running was a good way to cope with grief. With each step forward, I felt like I was moving towards something again. During the runs, I had time to think and process my emotions, which would change depending on the day. Some days I felt strong and other days I pulled my hat down lower to hide my tears. But I kept focused on my goal and the reasons why I wanted to run the marathon. I was running it for all of us: me, Joe, Jonah, and Jules. It was the demonstration of putting one foot in front of the other and moving forward when part of me wanted to curl up and let life go on without me. From the beginning of the training, I knew that I would be in a different place in seven months and it became a ray of hope.

As I walked towards the starting corral of the race, I was surrounded by a sea of runners, and it was emotional. I blinked away the tears as the National Anthem echoed over the loudspeakers. Fireworks lit up the pre-dawn sky. I gazed up at the city skyline and gave a big cheer with the rest of the crowd. Jumping up and down with excitement, I nervously clapped my gloved hands together. *No matter what,* I told myself, *you will finish this. I don't care how, but you will finish.* The gun shot rang out and we slowly made our way to the starting line. Fans lined the streets, cheering with banners and signs. I smiled to myself as I took my first step across the starting line and hit the 'start' button on my GPS watch.

I was slightly competitive when I was younger, but this time, I just felt thankful to be a part of the race. I took in the sights, observed the bystanders holding hand-made posters with clever statements like, 'If I see you collapse, I will pause your Garmin'. At times, I found myself smiling for no reason at all. Around mile eight, I started getting messages from my brother. To my surprise, he had requested to be at the marathon that morning at roll call. I kept an eye on the side of the road and spotted him in his uniform, standing at an intersection. I happily jogged over to give him a hug before continuing. I was touched that he'd come to support me. Laurel arrived as well and began texting me updates on other friends that were running the race.

At mile thirteen, the half marathoners took a sharp left turn, while the full marathon path continued straight ahead. A large construction sign stood on the side of the road and flashed instructions to the runners. It was a moment that I'd visualized many times during training. A large group of bystanders stood at the intersection, cheering for the marathoner runners as we made our way into the second half of the race. *I'm one of the full marathon runners*, I thought proudly to myself. I touched a necklace filled with Joe's ashes that I had tucked in my vest pocket. "'You're running this with me'", I reminded him. I knew the second half would bring challenges.

I thought back to a training run from the past summer. At the time, I'd completed fifteen miles and was nearing my house, feeling fatigued. In my mind, I saw myself as if I were outside of my body. Around me there were different versions of 'Gina' at various ages: elementary, teenage, twenties, and even older. I saw that all of them were helping propel me forward as if each step signified something more than just a physical run. 'Push' they kept yelling at me, 'Push harder'.

I saw waves of vibration shimmering around me as they strained to help me, and we advanced together as one group. I felt something shift inside of me as if an unseen threshold had been crossed. The image of their support stayed with me long after the run.

Now, as I passed the marker at mile twenty, I knew I'd finish the race. I felt good and tried to push myself more than usual. Normally I back off as soon as something becomes difficult, but I was determined to lay it all out on the line. I kept saying to myself, 'show them what you're made of' and pushing myself harder. I wanted to surprise anyone following my progress that I wasn't going to slow during that last hour.

At miles twenty-one and twenty-two, I held my pace but by mile twenty-three, I was starting to run out of steam. My legs grew heavy, and I began talking to Joe in my head. I knew he was with me, but I couldn't feel anything tangible. As we neared the final miles, I came into the part of town that was a few blocks from our first apartment. I remembered when we were dating and would run the same sidewalks with Bailey on a lead. Tears stung my eyes as I thought about how life had turned out for us. I could have never predicted the tragic turn of events. Feeling emotional and exhausted, I started asking Joe for a sign. 'Play Journey, play Grateful Dead, play *something*' I begged him, as I grew frustrated. *Why wasn't he sending me something?* In the past, when I demanded signs, they didn't show up, so I tried to put it out of my mind. After another half mile of silence, a text popped up on my watch from Laurel. I glanced down and read, "I feel like Joe is at the finish line cheering for you!" It boosted my spirits.

I thought I was going to break down the last mile, but I didn't. Feelings of grief didn't bubble up the way I expected;

if anything, the run really summed up my gratitude for all the help and support I had been given in the last year. I was grateful to have a healthy body that could participate and be a part of the race. It was amazing. I raised my hands overhead and grinned as I stepped over the finish line. Twenty-six miles. Tears sprang to my eyes as a woman stepped forward to place the bronze-colored medal around my neck. Another person wrapped a foil blanket around my shoulders as if I were a professional athlete. I had envisioned that moment so many times during training: on the good days and the dark ones. I picked up the medal to feel the weight of it between my fingers and looked at the crowd around me. It was a remarkable feeling of accomplishment.

The only missing piece was that Matt wasn't there to see me finish. I'd deliberately not asked him to come and watch. Joe had been closely tied to running and racing for me. I wanted to hide my grief from Matt. But as I crossed the finish line, I instinctively looked for him on the sidelines and felt a pang of disappointment. I realized that my fear had prevented me from allowing him into a day that my heart clearly wanted him to be a part of. I made a promise to myself that I wouldn't let it happen again.

Overall, the whole day felt special. From start to finish, it had an incredible feeling of light around it. I knew that it was blessed by those here on earth praying for me and those in spirit supporting me. I don't know how else to describe it. I know that even if I run other races, no race will ever compare with that one. It will always be one that I will want to go back to and re-live from start to finish; it truly was perfection. I laid down to nap that afternoon and as I closed my eyes, I felt Joe come forward to say he was proud of me. I smiled and fell into a restful sleep.

A few weeks after the marathon, I returned for an intuitive session with Sara. As soon as we started, she surprised me by asking if I felt Joe differently than I did when he first passed. It was something that had been weighing on my heart, but I hadn't mentioned it to anyone. I felt a deep sense of sadness, but I didn't know how to explain it. Something had distinctly changed since the marathon.

"I know he's there, but I don't *feel* him the same way I have for the last year. It's hard to describe, but it just feels different. Like he's not as close to me or something," I confessed to her. It had become rather *quiet,* and I had been struggling with how to come to peace with it.

She said my guides wished to come forward regarding this matter. She asked me what happened when I connected with an earthbound spirit. I explained to Sara that I usually feel love towards those in spirit but sometimes I felt irritation to match their energy. In the past, I've even fired off snippy replies like, 'I'm not going to sit and go back and forth with you on this all day. I've told you that you can go, the decision is yours'. It always makes me laugh afterwards, but I just go with it. The guides explained that sometimes I needed to lower my energy to reach out a hand to the those in spirit. If I stayed at the higher vibration, I'm not able to reach them as easily. The message resonated with me. I previously read that a common question is 'Why do spirits get stuck and need assistance in the first place'? A spiritual teacher explained that those on the lower frequency (human) can't experience the high vibrations of angels, guides, and ascended masters. In a way, the high vibration washes over them. However, if a human speaks, it catches their attention because it is closer to their vibration. Therefore, they 'hear' humans more easily than Divine beings. Sara went on to explain that just as I reached my hand down to those in spirit, Joe had lowered his vibration to resonate with me. He did so for as long as it was needed and then returned to the higher vibrational state. The timing made sense; he saw I was starting to walk on my own and the hands-on part was no longer needed. Although I understood the explanation logically, part of me felt inexplicably sad. It felt like the training wheels were coming off and I was learning to ride the bike on my own. A prospect that both comforted and scared me. After all, I wasn't even sure where the road was going. Little did I know, it would be months before the answer would come to me.

Chapter 17

My fingers nervously danced across the keyboard as I typed the words, 'One Light in the Dark- a spiritual blog about my journey through grief'. I shifted in my office chair and wondered if I was going to be able to go through with it.

It was Spring of 2020, amid the first wave of the COVID pandemic. The wheels of the world had grounded to a halt. I had been digging deep for several weeks, wrapped in a dark cocoon yet again. I knew I wanted to come out different on the other side. The nudge to start a blog had been growing and I realized I finally had something I wanted to say. In a meditation, I saw myself standing on a high dive with a crowd below cheering for me. I realized my guides were letting me know it was time to take that jump and for the first time, I felt ready.

I wrote a generic 'about me' section with the typical facts: single mom of two kids ages 9 and 11, etc. but the words felt inauthentic. *This shows nothing about who I really am,* I thought. I consulted Google about how to write a bio and saw that it was supposed to have a hook, something that made it different. Suddenly, I knew what I needed to say. Something that I had rarely told anyone.

"My name is Gina. I talk to dead people. Sometimes it may be someone's loved one, but that most often is not who I talk to. And yes, even though he is not an earthbound spirit, I talk to my husband. He has taught me valuable lessons and that our loved ones don't really leave us when they die."

I read it several times, pleased. It felt authentic. *Well, if anything, it checks the different box*, I thought to myself.

"Here goes nothing!" I said to myself, then hit the 'go live' button for the website. I wrapped my arms around myself and grinned at the computer screen - One Light in the Dark Blog was officially born. My Dad was one of the first people I sent it to. I sent the link to the website with the text, 'you may want to read this, I think you know the author'. A few minutes later my cell phone pinged.

"Congratulations! I'm proud of you," he responded. I felt like a child whose artwork was proudly displayed on the kitchen refrigerator.

"I started a blog about grief," I told Matt, on our Friday morning drive with coffee. I was still riding the wave of adrenaline.

"Oh my gosh, that's great! I'm so proud of you!" he said, with a smile before returning his eyes to the road. "Samantha had a blog about cooking. It was really good. She had followers and a cookbook-"

I glanced out the window and swallowed the lump in my throat. It felt like a comparison and my confidence deflated. *Of course, she had a blog*, I thought to myself. Some days I couldn't seem to move beyond her shadow.

"What can you tell me about it?" he asked, trying to engage me.

I hesitated, unsure of how much to disclose. I suddenly didn't want to continue the conversation out of fear. "Just my experience with grief. I really wrote it for myself, so I probably won't even have you read it or anything…" My words trailed off as I moved him back to arm's length. Inside, I knew I was being childish; I couldn't help but feel a bit bruised.

"Ok, I understand. But I would love to read it," he said, looking slightly confused, "when you're ready," he added.

At my next appointment, I recounted the story to my counselor, Aria. I tried to spin the story around Matt's response, but she saw the deeper concern.

"Did you tell him about the spiritual part, Gina?" Aria asked, ignoring my distraction tactics.

"Well…no," I said, as I shifted my weight on the couch. "But I told him it was about grief and spiritual."

"Did you say you talk to Joe and your spirit guides?" she asked.

"No, but he's going to freak out, Aria," I protested. In my head, I pictured Matt's Christian friends and family staging an intervention or glaring at me over dinner.

"You need to be honest with him. You aren't giving him the opportunity to respond. From what you've said he's very open on spiritual matters. I'm concerned you aren't really showing him the real you. This is a huge piece and you're not letting him see it. How can you be in an intimate relationship with someone who doesn't know the real you?" She waited for my response. I nodded and looked down at my hands, struggling with emotion.

"I just think it's a lot for people to take," I said, folding and unfolding my hands. "I know this isn't really about Samantha's blog," I said, with a sigh. I finally admitted my deeper fear, "What if he can't handle it? What if it's too much?"

"It sounds like everyone has been really supportive, whether they believe the same thing as you or not. How are you going to know unless you tell him?" she said, looking at me directly.

A few weeks later my fingers again nervously danced across the keyboard, but this time I was sending an email to Matt: 'I'm actually a little nervous sending this but I wanted to share it. I know my spiritual beliefs are a bit outside the normal. To be honest, it worries me sometimes that this will eventually be a problem for you. But I don't expect or want other people to believe what I do. I just think that to know me is to understand my deep devotion to God / The Divine. For some reason, that just presents differently for me. Trust me, I've asked God why I can't fit neatly in an organized religion like everyone else. But I think that's the nature of faith- trusting in something you can't prove but know in your heart to be true...for you. So here goes.' I attached one of my blog posts about finding joy in grief. In it, I quoted my spirit guides and mentioned that I talked to Joe in spirit. It was a big step, and I wasn't sure how he'd respond. I nervously kept an eye on my inbox. A few hours later, Matt sent a response. In his thoughtful manner, he told me the blog post was beautifully written and reassured me that my beliefs could be different from his. There was no trace of judgement or criticism; it was exactly the response I'd hoped for.

Slowly, I began to let more friends and family know about the blog. Most gave positive responses, and some gave no response at all. But no one challenged my beliefs or made derogative comments. I grew more comfortable and began writing blog posts on a weekly basis. I checked my webpage daily to look for new readers or comments and poured over the website analytics. Although I had a handful of readers, I didn't have many responses. My guides reminded me that it didn't matter if I had one reader or one million readers. They suggested I focus on the task at hand and let go of the belief, *Number of Followers = Success*. Gradually, I adjusted my expectations. Every time I completed a blog post and hit 'publish', I felt more like myself. But just as things were falling into place, my life took another unexpected turn.

Chapter 18

"**I**'m taking your mom to see a specialist," my dad told me, one afternoon. "Her counselor suggested she see a neurologist. He said that something seemed off with her walking. It reminded him of his father with Parkinson's."

"I did notice she lost her balance at Thanksgiving," I said, as the memory came back to me. She had been standing in my kitchen when she suddenly lost her balance and fell back into the refrigerator. A look of complete surprise came over her face, as if some imaginary person had walked up and pushed her. Months prior, she began to repeat a specific phrase in conversation. It sounded like a verbal tic, but she was unaware of it. I brought it up to the rest of the family, but no one acknowledged it. Other strange patterns began to emerge, but I felt like the family hypochondriac, who was always asking, 'Did you notice when Mom…' only to be met with blank faces.

"He seemed really interested in Grandpa's family history," my mom said, after the appointment. "He said based on my exam and history, it's chorea, a movement disorder."

"As in Huntington's Chorea?" I asked, a prickle of fear running down my spine.

Huntington's Chorea is a hereditary disease in my grandfather's side of the family. My grandfather had been tested in the 1990's when genetic testing was still in its infancy. The results came back negative, and we breathed a sigh of relief. He was diagnosed with Alzheimer's and spent his last days in a nursing home. Talk of Huntington's was quickly put to bed and rarely mentioned. It had remained as nothing more than a distant memory. Until now.

"Yes," she replied. "They think Grandpa was misdiagnosed."

My heart skipped a beat as I realized the implication of what she was telling me.

I told myself not to Google 'Huntington's Disease', but I found myself typing it in to the search bar as soon as we hung up. The results were nothing short of terrifying. Huntington's Chorea is a rare progressive neurological disease that causes the breakdown of nerve cells in the brain. Symptoms typically begin in mid-life and include movement disorders paired with severe cognitive and psychiatric issues. Most will spend the last years of their lives in an assisted living facility. I read online where one woman with a family history of HD called it, 'the cruelest disease on the planet'. I tried to remain positive, but my heart fell like a stone as I read how the disease affected her family. A few weeks later, I sat in on an appointment with the neurologist. He confirmed what I'd suspected, my mom had tested positive for the gene repeats that were the marker of Huntington's Disease. He got straight to the point.

"Barbara, given that you have the gene repeats and symptoms of chorea, we can diagnose late onset Huntington's Disease," he said, in a somber tone. "I'm sorry. As you know, your children will have a 50% chance of having the disease regardless of gender."

My parents were abnormally quiet about the results. I asked the doctor about genetic testing for myself and my siblings, and his response surprised me.

"I wouldn't recommend it," he said. "Partially for the psychological impact but also for insurance purposes. Once you've been diagnosed, you must disclose that information and it can be difficult to become insured. Additionally, you may test for the gene repeats, but not develop symptoms. So, testing isn't something I recommend. If you do pursue it, you would need to meet with a genetic and mental health counselor beforehand."

I thanked him for the information and wrote down the name of a specialist in the area. Coincidentally, one of the few Huntington's research centers was located less than thirty minutes away.

"It'll be OK, Mom," I told her, afterwards. She showed very little emotion, and I couldn't tell if it was denial, shock, or perhaps both. "We'll get through it," I said, trying to sound more confident than I felt.

I made a difficult call to my brother and sister. Although the three of us tried to remain positive, our minds were full of unanswerable questions. The implications were not only for ourselves but for our children and our children's children. The 'what if's' were overwhelming. What looked like a statistic on paper appeared very different in real life. In my mind, I saw the three of us standing in a row and being handed a quarter to flip. *In reality, isn't that what a 50% chance means?* I wondered. *If one of us tests positive, that person then hands the quarter to their children and so on. What does this mean for my family?*

I didn't sleep well for the next few days and was distracted when I joined Matt for coffee that week. How do you tell someone you're newly dating, 'Oh by the way, I may have a rare genetic disease?' I reluctantly explained the situation while he quietly listened. It sounded strange to say the words out loud as I explained the facts as best as I could. I told him that I'd understand if he wanted to just be friends. After losing his wife to cancer, he understood the gravity of what this could mean. I suggested he take some time to think it over, but he reminded me that nothing in life was guaranteed. He said he didn't need to think it about it and that he'd still choose to love me, even if I carried the gene. As much as I had come to know Matt's kind nature, his reaction still surprised me, and I felt lucky to be sitting beside him.

Unfortunately, the thought of Huntington's hung over my head like a black cloud. A few weeks later, I swore under my breath when my legs wobbled as I stepped back into a lunge on my yoga mat. I tried to brace my core and lift into a Crescent Lunge when I lost my balance and nearly toppled to the ground. My hand grazed the hardwood floor as I caught myself and rebalanced into the pose. I glanced at the video livestream in time to see that the in-studio participants had nailed the transition effortlessly.

It's early in the morning, I'm not warm yet, I told myself, but a little nagging voice in my head whispered, *why isn't it too early for them? They aren't falling over. Is it a sign? What if it's here?* I shoved the thought out of my mind and tried to refocus on my mat. I pushed my hands into the rubber surface of the mat and spread my fingers wide like I'd been taught, exhaling deeply.

Let it go, I told myself. Distracted, I brushed my hair out of my eyes and refocused. After a short time, I began to get lost in the meditative practice of movement and breath. By the time we reached Savasana at the end of class, the voice had quieted. But the word Huntington's lingered in the background of my mind, like a houseguest who'd overstayed their welcome. I found myself over analyzing my movement patterns. Suddenly a dropped glass held an ominous meaning. I told myself I was handling the news well, but inside it was eating away at me.

One afternoon, I was sitting with Kelley, Deb, Laurel, and Whitney in a garage. Due to Covid, we spaced the patio lounge chairs in a large circle. I carried in a green juice and explained that I wasn't drinking due to a detox. They nodded and went back to their glasses of wine without question. We laughed and caught up on the latest news for a few hours. When I stood to leave, I lost my balance and stutter-stepped forward, barely catching myself. I saw a questioning look cross Laurel's face. Inside, I started to panic. *Oh my God*, I thought. *It's happening. Is this the first symptom?* My stomach was in knots on the drive home. I made the kids dinner and tried to ignore the story that was running in the back of my mind.

The next morning, I called my guides and Joe forward for advice. I was terrified of what Huntington's could mean for their future. Joe came forward and said he was holding us close. He told me not to worry about the kids and that they would be fine. I breathed a sigh of relief and felt comforted by his words. I remembered that researchers were close to developing new treatments so even if our children carried the gene, they might not experience symptoms. I saw how my anxiety could be creating the perceived symptoms. My spirit guides wouldn't confirm whether I had the gene but reminded me to focus on the present. I told myself that I couldn't control the next week, but I could focus on the day in front of me. My anxiety didn't fade overnight, but I began to consciously turn my thoughts away from it until it diminished. Once again, I was reminded of the vision of the ship. I knew there was more I wanted to accomplish but I needed to figure out where I wanted to go. I began brainstorming what I wanted, and the answer came to me one day during meditation.

Chapter 19

"Thank you for signing up for Balancing Moods," a woman with dark hair and an accent said. I nervously adjusted the volume on my laptop. "Let's go around and introduce ourselves. Please state where you're from and where you are in your yoga journey."

I anxiously waited for my turn as I listened to the other students give their backgrounds. Most were practicing yoga teachers having completed the 200-hour certification requirement. I was the only one that wasn't currently teaching.

"I started taking yoga teacher classes about five years ago, but then life got busy, and I didn't finish it. I'm back because I want to teach a workshop on grief, and I want yoga to be a part of it. I don't know if I'll teach classes or not," I said, in a rush.

The idea for a grief workshop had come to me a few weeks before, during a meditation. I realized I wanted to offer self-care techniques to those who were grieving. Once the idea formed, I became excited about it. I sketched out a rough outline of what I wanted the workshop to look like. I knew I'd need to prepare before stepping into the role of instructor.

Although my confidence was building from writing, I wasn't ready to face an entire room of people. Due to the global pandemic, yoga certification classes were being offered online, which allowed me to attend.

"That's a great idea. I'm sure that will be helpful," the teacher responded.

I nodded and tried to ignore the uncomfortable feeling inside. I had purposely left out part of my story and pretended like I had never taught a yoga class. My prior teaching experience was not something I shared with many people. Years before, I completed three yoga instructor classes and was approved to teach yoga without having a full certification. Although I'd been doing yoga regularly, I was never an advanced student. Back then, I was hired to be a part-time instructor in an apartment complex. During my first class, I mixed up the routine and cued a pose incorrectly. I panicked and lost my place in the movement sequence. I stumbled over my words and was mortified. I wanted to run from the room and never come back. Later, I learned this happens to almost every new yoga teacher, but I set a standard for myself that was unreachable. I taught a handful of classes that summer, but my nerves kept getting the best of me. Several of the young women in the complex would practice their own routine during class, which I found distracting. *Did they not like me? Was I teaching poorly?* I felt insecure, and as a result, I began to dread Saturday mornings. A ball of anxiety would grow in my stomach as the weekend neared. I would wake up hours before the class to review the poses. Eventually, I told Joe that it was too demanding and bowed out of the position, too ashamed to admit the truth. Now, as part of the online course, we were required to give live demonstrations.

"Ok, Gina. It's your turn. Why don't you walk us through Child's pose," the instructor asked.

My mind went blank, and I realized I had no idea how to cue a basic pose. Although I had continued to practice yoga occasionally, I hadn't been to a formal class in years.

"Ummm… extending our arms forward and pushing back. Feeling the extension in the back…" My mind raced. *How do they cue this pose?* "Reaching forward. Breathing deeply." I fell silent, praying the instructor would take pity on me.

"That's fine," she said, curtly, when she realized I wasn't giving any other instruction. "Maybe next time you could focus on the expansion of the back body and use more descriptive language." Her mouth turned down slightly and I could tell she was displeased. I felt my cheeks redden. "Ok," she sighed, audibly. "Who's next?"

Although I found the coursework interesting, my confidence was shaken. I fumbled again in the next weekend course. One student seemed especially irritated at my ineptness. She was an attractive woman with long black hair who owned a yoga studio on the West Coast. Every time I went to speak, she would give the slightest roll of the eyes and it rattled my nerves. Doubts crept in and I began to question my decision to start back into classes. The other students seemed so polished and well spoken. *Maybe I wasn't meant to be a yoga teacher*, I thought, as the familiar story of self-doubt settled in.

I sat down one morning to review the curriculum for my course track, and realized the classes I'd signed up for were *post-certification* courses. Most of the students had already completed the 200, 300, and even 500-hour Yoga Teacher certification programs. Several owned their own studios and had been teaching for a decade or more. I hadn't even completed the 200-hour course. Mapping out classes in a notebook, I realized I could finish my certification in a few months. The following morning, I called the school and asked to re-take the Level One class. I knew I needed to rebuild my foundation as a teacher. The Level One class arrived a few weeks later and it was a completely different experience. The instructor was friendly and encouraging to new students.

"You really nailed that," a fellow student said, after one of my demonstrations. "I don't want to go now, I won't be any good," she laughed.

"Thanks," I said, feeling pleased. "But this is my second time through Level One. Don't worry, there's no judgement. You'll do great."

"Why didn't you stick with teaching?" she asked me later, while we were on a break.

"To be honest? I let my nerves get to me. I thought I had to be perfect and forgot why I wanted to teach in the first place. I don't want to teach in a yoga studio - that's not where I fit in. I always wanted to teach beginners."

The teacher of the Level One class left a distinct impression on me. She talked openly about how yoga helped her through addiction and the grief of losing a parent to suicide. I was surprised to learn someone else's life had similarities to mine. I also saw how she allowed students to connect with her by being vulnerable. Her class gave me the confidence to approach a local yoga center about hosting the grief workshop. I explained my idea to combine yoga and meditation along with self-care tips during grief. To my delight, they liked the idea and we set a date on the calendar. I prepared for the workshop for weeks, but the owner of the yoga center surprised me by asking to cancel the event.

"We don't have anyone signed up right now," the owner said, apologetically. "And someone else wants to rent the space, so…"

"Oh…Ok," I agreed, reluctantly. Inside I wanted to request a few more days, but instead I hung up, frustrated.

I rarely post on Facebook group forums, but I'd been closely following a private group for a Shamanic course I was taking to connect with nature. The course was led by Sandra Ingerman, a world-renowned Shaman. The FB group posts were mainly between students commenting on the coursework and the administrator of the page. Before I could talk myself out of it, I posted about my situation. I wrote about how I lost my husband to suicide and had wanted to host a workshop to help others with self-care in grief. I explained how my event was cancelled at the last minute and shared my deep disappointment at not being able to lead the event. I asked the community for advice. The response I received from this group was incredibly supportive.

One woman shared the story of how she lost her baby and decided to form a six-week support group. Every week, she waited for someone to show up, but no one ever came to the group. She had no regrets and said the lessons she learned through the experience were ultimately healing. I couldn't imagine the courage it took to show up week after week and sit in an empty room. Somehow, that made the story even more inspiring. Then to my surprise, Sandra Ingerman responded to me directly. She told me with complete certainty that I had to put on the workshop, even if I presented it to an empty room.

"Show the universe that you followed through and that you are showing up," she wrote. "I've been teaching for over twenty years, and this is what you must do. I promise if you do this, the next time you'll have participants."

A woman in the group sent me a private message on FB and offered to be a participant via zoom. She said she'd been struggling with grief and thought the workshop would be helpful. I stepped out of my comfort zone and agreed.

On the day of the event, I nervously got on the zoom link and introduced myself. I briefly explained my journey into grief, then asked her who she was grieving for.

"I lost my two beloved dogs in the last year," she said tearfully.

I paused for a moment, caught by surprise. I'd been expecting the loss of a friend or loved one. But then I remembered how it felt to lose my dog, Bailey, and how deeply I grieved for him. I realized the emotion of grief didn't change depending on the relationship. I took a breath and began to lead the workshop as planned. At the end, I even included a twenty-minute yoga routine.

"How long have you been teaching yoga?" she asked, as we wrapped up.

"Actually, I don't. I'm finishing classes for a teaching certification," I confided.

"Wow, I would never have guessed," she said. "You seemed very comfortable." I grinned and thanked her. A few months later, I surprised myself by completing my 200-hour certification; something I would never have predicted a few years before.

Suddenly I was back to being a teacher- a role I still wasn't fully comfortable with, but I pushed forward and signed up to lead a few small classes at a local spa's event center. My second week, I taught three students. I encouraged them to have fun and laughed at myself when I fell out of the tree pose. It wasn't perfectly guided, but I didn't allow myself to be discouraged. At the end of the class, I led a guided meditation from a book, while the students were lying on their backs with their eyes closed. During the meditation, students were directed to place their worries into the basket of an imaginary hot air balloon. Then they were instructed to cut the ropes one by one and allow the balloon to fly away. As I described the balloons rising up into the air, a strange sensation came over me. The hair on my arms and the back of my neck began to rise as if an imaginary wind had risen from the floor. I glanced up at the students, confused, before realizing what was happening. I was sensing the energy of their imaginary balloons taking flight.

"Oh my gosh," I thought to myself. "This is working- they're actually releasing!" I was amazed. I quickly looked back down at the book and finished the mediation. Afterwards, a young woman approached me.

"Thank you for class," she said. She turned to leave then paused. "I liked your approach; you were really nice. In other classes, they didn't do that," her voice caught for a moment, and I realized she was close to tears. "Thank you." She looked embarrassed, and quickly walked away. I was touched and it reminded me why I wanted to become a yoga teacher.

A few months later, I visited a local wellness center and began talking with the owner. To my surprise, I found myself telling her how I was a Reiki Master and asked if I could rent a room at their location to see clients. She agreed and I began by offering free reiki sessions to the owner and the staff. The sessions were well received, and I grew excited to see outside clients.

During the first sessions with new clients, I found myself a bit apprehensive about using my intuition. One day I had a hand placed over a woman's belly when I felt, intuitively, she had lost a child. I felt the urge to share this information but hesitated. Suddenly I was back in a memory from years before.

"I think there are spirits present," someone said. We were standing in a small massage room.

I was one of seven people participating in a 'Reiki Share', which is where reiki practitioners take turns performing reiki on each other. Reiki shares are often helpful to new practitioners and participants are encouraged to share intuitive feedback during the sessions.

A woman was lying on a massage table, resting with her eyes closed. Valerie, a senior Reiki practitioner, was directing the group while the rest of us stood around the table with our hands gently resting on or above the participant.

"Why aren't they going into the light?" someone asked.

"It's the spirit of a boy. He's angry at his father who abused him," Valerie said, keeping her hands resting under the woman's head.

I closed my eyes and tuned in to my intuition. I'd already recognized the spirits of the boy and his father, but I didn't feel animosity between the son and father. Quite the opposite; I felt the father had made amends with the son and there was only love between them. A feeling of forgiveness and understanding flooded my senses.

"I'm not quite getting any anger," I said, hesitantly. "I think he's fine. He-"

"Oh, the boy is definitely angry at the father," Valerie said, cutting me off.

"But..." I tried to explain.

"Oh yes, Valerie. I agree, he hates him," someone else chimed in, and others began to follow suit.

"Lots of anger."

I felt like a crazy person in the room as I glanced around at the others. *Why are they not getting this?* I wondered.

"Let's have the angels take him to the Light," Valerie said, confidently.

The others turned their focus to the unseen beings, while I stood there confused.

Wait, why am I automatically wrong? Why aren't we discussing another possibility? I thought to myself. I turned my attention back to the participant and sent energy to where I felt it was most needed. I swallowed my opinion, but unanswered questions began to turn over in my mind.

Years later, back with my own client, as I stood with my hands over her abdomen, I realized I had a choice to make even though I was conflicted. Did I express my truth or remain quiet?

I don't know this woman and maybe she never lost a baby. I'm going to lose all credibility if I just blurt that out! What if she gets angry? I was sharing my doubts with my guides, but the nudge continued to grow stronger.

"Gina, if you're going to do this, then *do* this," one of my guides prompted.

"So... do you have any children?" I asked, figuring I could ease towards the bigger question.

"Yes, I have four," She said. *Four?* I thought. *That's a lot of kids. I'm completely off base.* But I took a deep breath and figured, it didn't hurt to ask.

"Well, this may sound odd, but I feel a baby's presence. Does that mean anything to you?" Then I held my breath.

"Yes, it does. I miscarried a few months ago," she replied.

"I'm sorry," I said, then added tentatively, "I believe it's a little girl and she's letting you know she's still with you in spirit." Much to my surprise, more information came tumbling out of my mouth. I took a deep breath and realized I felt more at ease after delivering the message. I looked at the client to see her reaction, but she didn't look upset. After the session, she said that she took comfort in knowing her daughter was still with her. As I continued to receive validations from more of my clients, my confidence began to grow. I began to trust myself and delivered messages, even when they didn't quite make sense to me. But I also remembered how vulnerable

I was after Joe's death, and I didn't want anyone to feel the way I did when Valerie told me Joe's message was false. As a result, I discussed intuition with clients prior to each session.

'Sometimes, I get intuitive messages' I would say, 'but it's important to remember the information is coming through my filter, so please take only what resonates with you. If I say something that feels off, then disregard it. Always trust *your* intuition first'. As months went by, I saw an improvement in my skills as an intuitive and energy healer.

I was sitting at my computer one day when I opened an email from the wellness center to find they had featured me as a reiki practitioner. Delighted, I forwarded the email to a few people, including Matt. I could tell he was genuinely proud of me and I began to share more about my work with them.

As my business grew, I began to study other modalities and brought new healing tools into the reiki sessions. Eventually, I purchased a large bag to carry a variety tuning forks, divination cards, and various crystals. Wanting to share my new 'tools', I invited the local medium, Sara, over to my house for ceremonial cacao. She was sitting at my kitchen table one afternoon, as I poured both of us a cup of cacao, explaining that it is pure chocolate from the cacao bean.

"I don't know exactly how others do it, but this is what I do," I said, as I demonstrated how to set the space for ceremony.

"This is amazing," she responded. "I love it."

"I just feel like there needs to be something more out there," I said to her. "There are so many things that could make people feel better, like cacao ceremony or different daily rituals. I feel like it would help a lot of people."

"Well, I've always wanted to lead a retreat. Why don't we team up and do it together?" she said.

"Really?" I grinned. She made it sound so simple.

"Why not?" she responded. "I love all the things that you're showing me. We should start hosting retreats."

"I would love that," I said, growing excited as the thought began to take shape. "We could offer cacao ceremony, yoga, and meditation!" We eagerly began discussing what the retreat might look like and a few hours later, I felt slightly drunk on adrenaline and cacao.

"Are we really going to do this?" I asked, as she opened her car door to leave.

"Believe it," she exclaimed, as she shut the door behind her. Then she leaned out the window and said, "Can't you feel the energy?"

A few months later, Sara and I purchased plane tickets for Mt. Shasta, California and arranged to stay in a Bed and Breakfast. I was shocked that I'd managed to pull off the trip. I explained to Matt that we were looking for possible retreat locations, but this was only partially true; something in my soul longed to step foot on Mt. Shasta. It was a feeling that I couldn't put into words. In spiritual circles, Mt. Shasta is a place of myths and legends. There were stories of off planet beings that resided in the mountain, energetic vortexes, and miracles on sacred land. In the weeks leading up to the trip, I was excited to see what magic would unfold on the trip. But as the flight neared, I began to feel something else too; inexplicably, I felt like I was going home.

Chapter 20

The days leading up to the trip were overloaded as I struggled to coordinate the kids' schedules with Matt and my parents. I felt guilty and overwhelmed at the thought of leaving them for five days. More than once, I considered backing out of the trip. *Maybe it's not the right time*, I thought to myself. However, I knew I'd regret missing the opportunity to go to one of my dream destinations, so I moved forward with the plans. As I settled into my airplane seat, I knew I had made the right decision. The trip across the country took multiple flights followed by a three-hour car ride. Sara and I were both surprised by how smoothly the day of travel transpired. It seemed like everyone we met was friendly and we enjoyed ourselves. I felt strangely energized as I watched the California landscape roll past the window of the rental car that afternoon.

When we arrived at the Bed and Breakfast, we learned that the owner had been called away for an emergency. On the front porch, our names were displayed on a chalkboard under a sign that read 'Welcome'. To my surprise, the front door stood wide open to allow in the mountain air. Two guests offered to show us around the older home and helped us settle in. That evening, Sara and I wrapped ourselves in large, fluffy blankets and sat outside in lounge chairs. The back patio overlooked a small stream decorated with delicate ceramic houses, creating a fairy village. I took in the view as we talked with the other guests well into the evening. As daylight faded, fairy lights twinkled over the stream while a clear view of Mt. Shasta rose in the distance. The scene was so picturesque that I almost couldn't believe I was there.

That night, I settled into my bed to go to sleep, exhausted after the day of travel. I curled up, feeling peaceful. Just as I was drifting off to sleep, I became aware of three beings standing near the fireplace. I startled awake, feeling unsure as to what just happened. I laid awake for a few minutes before I started to doze off a second time. Suddenly, there they were again - three beings standing shoulder to shoulder. I shot up in bed and turned on the light, but the room was empty. I laid back down, wondering what was going on. Nothing else happened and finally, I grew tired and fell asleep until morning.

The next day, I woke up early and made breakfast in the little kitchen. The other guests left for the day, so we had the house to ourselves. Sara and I settled in at the large dining room table overlooking the backyard and decided to hold a cacao ceremony. As I sipped my cup of cacao, I told Sara about the visit from the three beings the previous night. She calmly nodded as if this were an everyday occurrence.

"I'm kind of jealous," she laughed. "I wish I'd spiritual visitors last night. Do you think it was the Lemurians?" The area of Mt. Shasta is reported to be deeply connected to the ancient civilization of Lemuria. Some say that the Lemurians were advanced spiritual beings who lived in balance with the earth. During the downfall of Atlantis and Lemuria, the Lemurians moved underground, and some believe, they still reside inside Mt. Shasta.

"I don't know," I said, with a shrug. "There were definitely three beings in the room. Both times they were standing very close together."

We talked a few minutes more before turning our attention back to the development of a retreat. We titled the retreat and described our general concept. I explained that I wanted to help people reconnect with their hearts and nature. I offered ideas for activities and outlined what messages I felt called to share with others. We fell deeply into a flow state and the morning hours sped by. We finally drew the session to a close several hours later in the early afternoon and decided to head out to the surrounding area. I was curious to experience the energy of Mt. Shasta in person. Silently, I took in the surroundings as we drove away from the town. Towering pine trees lined the two-lane road as we wound our way up the mountain

I was eager to reach the summit, but a gate blocked the road a few miles before Panther Meadow. We pulled into a parking spot and walked over to the large map posted at a trailhead. A sign hung near the map stating the main road to Mt. Shasta was closed. A small group of hikers milled around, discussing how to proceed. We walked up and joined them, looking curiously at the map but there were no other roads to reach Panther Meadow.

I tried to ignore the sting of disappointment as we climbed back into the car and began to head down the mountain. *Why would I be led to Shasta and not be able to visit the actual mountain? This doesn't make sense.* I grew quiet in my thoughts. It wasn't as hard for me to let go of my disappointment since

I didn't really understand what I was missing. I'd never been here before. I tried to look at it from a positive angle and figured it just wasn't meant to be. Sara, however, would not be so easily deterred. Once we returned to the Bed and Breakfast, she busied herself on her phone. She called the Park Ranger Station to inquire about the closure. I chuckled when I realized what she was up to. They explained the road was still closed from the winter season.

"The crews haven't been able to clear the road of debris, so it's not passable by car," a Ranger explained.

"But how do I get to Panther Meadow?" Sara demanded.

"Take the road," the Ranger replied.

"Take the road?" she asked, unconvinced.

"Take the road," he said, in a matter-of-fact tone. "Walk around the gate and head up the road, two miles to Panther Meadow."

Sara burst out laughing and hit herself on the forehead. "Of course. Tomorrow, we can just walk up the road to the entrance."

The forecast was calling for colder weather the following day and although we'd had mild weather that afternoon, now evening was approaching, the wind was picking up considerably. Heavy, gray clouds rolled in, and the temperature was dropping. I despised being cold and I tried to break it to Sara that I might not be up for the hike the following day. We agreed to wait and see what the weather looked like.

I woke up the next morning as a howling wind whipped through the windows of the inn. Although it was warm inside, the wind sounded foreboding. I looked out and saw dark, cloudy skies with icy rain. I dragged myself into the tiny shower and opened the circular window to disperse the steam. I breathed in the mountain air as I dried my hair. In the distance, Mt. Shasta kept catching my eye. Maybe I wasn't meant to visit the mysterious mountain after all.

'Gina, you're being silly,' a voice in my head said. 'You've run in far colder weather than this! Are you going to come this far and let a little poor weather stop you?' I realized that deep inside I wanted to at least try to get up the mountain. I came back to my room and found a text from Sara saying the weather looked too bad to attempt the mountain hike. I immediately felt disappointment. To my surprise, I responded that if she was willing to try, I was. We headed out that afternoon, with me wearing every piece of clothing from my suitcase: three layers of yoga pants and sweatshirts under my windbreaker. I wished I'd thought to pack gloves and a hat, but I'd expected mild weather in May.

We pulled up to the gate and parked at the base of the mountain. The skies were a brilliant blue and the sun was shining. The bitter wind was relentless as we started up the mountain road, but the scenery was distracting from the cold. Green pine trees lined the road along with white snow piles not yet melted from the spring sun. We were the only people on the road, and I was surprised at how much I enjoyed the walk. We talked the entire way, stopping occasionally to take pictures. I was telling Sara about my experience of the marathon and how I loved reading the spectators' signs. Just as I finished the story, we came across rocks in the road that spelled out the sentence, 'can it get any better than this', and we both laughed at the perfect timing.

As the wooden sign for Panther Meadow appeared, we felt a sense of accomplishment. Halfway up the path, I paused when I caught the sound of faint drumming in the distance. We had only seen one other person the entire way up the mountain, yet there it was – the soft beat of drums echoing in the valley.

"Wait, do you hear that?" I asked, a few minutes later when I heard another strange sound. I tilted my head to the side, "It sounds like horses." We quickly traced the sound to the small stream bubbling next to us. We continued to make our way slowly up the steep hill, at times having to clamor over three-foot snowbanks. There was no distinct path to follow, and it felt like we were wandering alone in the forest.

"Are you sure this is the right way?" I asked, repeatedly, wondering if we were lost. "Have we reached it?"

"Trust me, you'll know it when you see it," Sara said.

Eventually, the trees parted, and we found ourselves at the edge of a large, open meadow. Mt. Shasta towered in the background and the mountains created a ridge around the horizon. We paused in the meadow, and I suggested we do a form of a sun salutation to honor the land.

"We honor Father Sky" I led, as we extended our arms upward. "We honor Mother Earth" as we bent and placed our hands on the cold ground. Then we made our way across the alpine meadow. The air felt so thick with energy that I fought the urge to politely say, 'I'm sorry, excuse me. Can I get through'? We carefully made our way to where the Clear Creek headwater. A small pool of water bubbled out of the earth and trickled across the field. We gazed out across the green meadow in reverence.

I took out Joe's ashes from the same necklace that I'd carried with me during the marathon. Sara knew I was planning on placing them in a special spot. I had felt Joe with me closely in the weeks leading up to the trip and I found myself talking about him frequently to Sara. Being out West and in nature brought back memories of our hikes in Las Vegas, Nevada. We felt especially close on those trips. One day, we made a half day hike with only two Gatorades and Twix Bars. We scrambled over boulders and talked the entire way up the mountain. A seasoned hiker looked at us like we were crazy when we joined him on the summit. He commented that we weren't carrying backpacks or extra water. The next year, we returned prepared with backpacks, emergency gear, and even walking sticks. I knew Joe would have loved Mt. Shasta. Although he was experiencing it through my eyes, I missed seeing him physically standing next to me.

"My love will always flow like this river," I said, out loud, as I tipped my necklace to spill the ashes gently into the pool below.

An unexpected wave of grief welled up and a sob rose in my throat. I swallowed hard. I hadn't expected it to feel like a goodbye and yet it did. Sometimes it feels like there are a million good-byes in grief.

I took a deep breath and tried to bring my emotions back under control. After a few minutes, I wiped my eyes and went to re-join Sara. We faced the open meadow and marveled at the beauty. I felt my heart open and honored to be standing on the land. Suddenly, the air looked hazy in the field. In my mind's eye, I saw a man with a large, feathered headdress step forward.

"Umm... is it just me," I said quietly, "or did an Indian Chief just step forward in spirit?"

"Oh my gosh, just as you were saying that I saw him too," she exclaimed. I worried he might consider us trespassers, but I quickly realized he wasn't angry with us. He came forward and gave us his blessing. I felt deeply honored to be standing with the ancestors and mentally told him so.

"Do you realize we can hear birds now? It was quiet before." Sara said. I realized she was right. Despite the numerous trees, we hadn't heard one bird on our walk up the mountain, yet the air was now filled with song.

"He said the moon came closer to the Earth to witness our return," Sara said, referring to a past life. We looked up and saw the moon in the blue sky with white clouds fanning around it. We had noticed it earlier that day and even taken pictures of it.

As we prepared to leave, we gave thanks to the ancestors. Then we tried to delicately follow the creek back to the main path, but it was difficult. The wind was picking up and it was starting to steadily snow. Sara suggested we cut across the field so we could reach the main road more quickly, but I worried the ancestors would find this disrespectful to the land.

"I really don't want to piss off an Indian Chief, but OK," I said, reluctantly, when I saw the winds were not dying down. Gray clouds began blotting out the sun and the snowflakes swirled around us with the wind. "At least, they can see our hearts and know we don't mean any disrespect," I said, as I nervously made my way through the meadow.

"The Chief says, 'noted and appreciated'," Sara said. I burst out laughing as I realized he was teasing me. 'Noted and appreciated' was something Sara often said.

"He stole your line," I giggled.

Did an Ancient Indian Chief just tease me? I thought to myself in amazement. As soon as we reached the road, the sky opened, and the snowfall grew more intense. The wind was formidable, and we made our way as quickly as we could down the mountain. I smiled to myself despite the bitter cold. I couldn't imagine having the same experience if we'd simply driven up the mountain in a warm car. Part of what made it special was the effort it required and the true connection with nature. We returned to the warm Bed and Breakfast feeling like we'd had a great adventure. The owner had returned to the home and offered to light the bedroom fireplaces. After dinner, we sat around a fireplace and marveled at the day. Sara took out her phone and looked up information on Panther Meadow.

She read aloud, "It says here that the Native Americans believe the land is protected by the Spirit of Chief Skell." She paused and looked up from the phone.

"So, you're saying we saw the spirit of an Indian Chief in Panther Meadow and he *actually* has a name?" I asked, incredulous. "Who else could that be?"

We both sat in stunned silence for a moment then I had her read the paragraph again.

"That's incredible," was all I could say.

That night as I laid in bed and watched the flames flicker in the fireplace, the room filled with a warm glow. I felt like a small child on Christmas Day. I didn't want to close my eyes out of fear that it might be a dream. The following morning, I sat down in the quiet house with my cup of coffee and guidebook of Mt. Shasta. It was the last day of the trip, and we would be leaving Mt. Shasta to drive to Sacramento in the afternoon. We planned to stay in a hotel close to the airport to be ready for the early flight the following morning.

I sipped my coffee and opened the guidebook to find a stunning picture of Castle Crag. I remembered we'd driven past Castle Crag on the way to town. When the car came around a bend, a towering mountain of rock had suddenly loomed in the distance. Its momentous size was impressive and there was something other worldly about the gray stone. I read the description in the guidebook, intrigued. Some believed it was connected to the legend of Lemuria. The author noted visitors could receive a blessing from the land and I knew what I wanted to do that day. As soon as Sara woke up, I asked if we could visit Castle Crag.

As we drove up a winding mountain road, I examined the map of trails, then glanced at Sara. The one that I wanted to do was rated 'very difficult'. I wasn't sure we were prepared for the hike, so we agreed to check out the more popular section of Castle Crag first. We continued driving on a narrow road through a heavily wooded area. We located a small parking lot and walked to a clearing through the dense pine forest. I stopped and looked up at Castle Crag in the distance. Although the scenery was beautiful, I longed to be deeper in the forest. I made an offering of cacao to the land and said a silent prayer to receive a blessing from the land. I felt privileged simply to be standing in that spot in nature. We were walking back to the car when my eye caught sight of another path on the far end of the parking lot. The trail headed into an even denser part of the forest and immediately, I felt drawn to it. I walked over and read the trail sign, only to realize this was the path on the map that I had been debating earlier. I suggested we try it, even though it was labeled as 'very difficult'.

As we hiked, I could feel the sun beginning to set and I became nervous. I thought back to when Joe and I were in our early thirties and rented a cabin a few hours away from Columbus. We didn't tell anyone; we just left the city and drove to the southern part of the state. We reached the cabin in the late afternoon and decided to go for a quick run on the nearby trail. We glanced at the map but didn't take it with us and we left our cell phones because we figured we'd be back in an hour. We started in the direction of the trail at a casual jogging pace; leaving the parking lot behind, the woods closed in around us.

"Isn't this cool?" Joe exclaimed.

"It's so different than running at home," I agreed.

I matched his pace as I took in the lush greenery around me. We followed small white flames painted on the tree trunks and made jokes about the white blazes. A light rain started to fall which felt refreshing as we ran. We both grew quiet; the only sound was our breathing and the rain cascading down on the leaves. The outside world seemed distant as I focused on Joe's back in front of me. We talked easily but, as the run continued, we began to tire. I was unprepared for the elevation of the hills, and we took more frequent walk breaks. After a while, the trails began to run together, and we no longer saw the white flames on the trees to let us know we were on the right path. I grew worried; surely, we had gone a few miles, where was the turn off to the car?

"How much further do you think?" I asked Joe. I suddenly regretted not bringing the map or my phone.

"Not far," he said. "I think we've gone about five miles, although it's hard to tell with the elevation." The hills were larger than anything I'd seen, yet we were climbing them with ever more urgency. But at the top of each hill, we were always greeted by another one. We both became aware that we hadn't seen anyone for miles, and it was starting to get dark. We continued climbing hill after hill, and I began seeing spots floating across my vision. Joe assured me it was nothing, but I saw a look of concern flash in his eyes. He began to casually ask about my vision at timed intervals. I knew he was medically assessing me and finally asked what he was concerned about.

"I think it's a sign of dehydration. We'll get back soon, and you'll need to drink extra water," he advised, in an overly calm voice. I could tell he wasn't telling me everything.

My legs began to feel extremely fatigued as daylight faded. We heard large groups of birds settling in for the night. We discussed what would happen if we were forced to spend the night in the woods. We guessed the time to be 9pm which meant we'd been on the trail for over four hours. We started to follow white blazes on the trees, but we began to question if we were following the right trail markers; something didn't feel right.

"I just want something to eat and drink! I'm exhausted," I complained.

"I know G. We'll find it," he said, trying to sound confident. We looked around for any signs of other people or houses but there was only forest. "Maybe we got turned off on a horse trail," Joe said, more to himself. "If only we had the map, I could figure it out."

The white blazes became nearly impossible to see in the dark. I tried to adjust to the reality that we were likely going to spend the night in the woods. I knew it would be uncomfortable but what concerned me most was the fact that when daylight did arrive, we would *still* be lost. I prayed for my grandfather to intervene. As time passed, I prayed more fervently. 'Please, Grandpa. Help us find a way out, *now*'.

Suddenly, I saw something twinkle in the distance and squinted into the forest. "Is that a light?" I asked.

Joe and I both stared hard into the darkness. We could just make out a secondary path that cut through the woods and decided to chance it. We figured in the worst case, it might lead to a house, and we could ask for help. We were both surprised when the tree line opened to a dimly lit parking lot. The lot was empty except for an old black convertible sitting under the only light.

"Is that our car?" I asked, in partial disbelief.

We rushed towards the car as if it might disappear like a mirage. Relief washed over me as I sank into the worn leather seat. Back at the cabin, we eased into the hot tub to soak our sore muscles and laughed about how close we came to sleeping outside.

"That seriously felt as hard as a full marathon," Joe laughed. "Those hills were brutal." We estimated that we'd covered at least ten miles of trail running. We joked that we'd never been more grateful for a bed to sleep in for the night.

Now, as I continued the climb at Castle Crag, that memory came back to me clearer than it had in years. Sara and I ran into a group of hikers coming back down the mountain, which broke me out of my memories.

"How much further is it?" we asked.

"It's pretty far. We headed out early this morning and you still have at least an hour or two to go. You won't be able to get up the rocks at the end without equipment."

After the hikers had carried on their way, I turned to Sara with concern.

"I think we should turn around. It's getting late and we still have to drive to the hotel." I glanced at the sky trying to gauge how quickly darkness would fall. It was hard to determine through the dense forest, but I could sense the late afternoon sun beginning to soften.

"We can make it," she said, but I held firm. I didn't want to be stuck in the forest overnight when we had a flight the next morning. Reluctantly, she agreed, and we turned around and started heading back down the path. As we walked, I tried to picture the Lemurian people in the woods, secretly hoping that I'd see one of them. I'd been casually scanning the trees hoping to see a flutter of white movement. I felt like a child trying to catch a glimpse of an elf at Christmastime. *Crack!* A branch snapped nearby, and my stomach lurched in excitement. I looked closer to see the brown flash of a squirrel's tail scurry into the underbrush. My heart sank, and I chided myself for expecting too much.

After we'd walked for a few minutes in silence, Sara commented, "Your guides say you're feeling gipped. This wasn't quite what you hoped for."

I found myself struggling to explain what I was feeling. I felt somewhat selfish complaining after such a magical trip.

"I don't know," I said, hesitantly. "I guess a little bit."

I looked around the woods as we walked into an area where the trees grew thicker. It was vibrant and green, and the air suddenly felt different. The temperature dropped a few degrees, and the path was deeply shaded by trees.

"What is it you need to do? Your guides are asking," Sara said.

I looked around again and sighed. "Can we just sit for a few minutes?" I wasn't ready to leave the forest and I could feel something pulling at my heart.

"Sure," she replied, "but where?" We both looked around as if a park bench was going to appear.

"I don't know. How about right here?" I pointed to the side of the trail next to us. I stepped to the side and sat down on the rocks.

She sat down next to me without complaint. I gazed at the forest in front of me. The ground was dense with fallen trees and leaves. We both took in the scene for a few minutes then Sara encouraged me to use my intuition.

"So, what do you see?"

I gave a big sigh as I closed my eyes.

"Nothing," I replied.

"Just say what comes to mind- anything," she encouraged.

I tried to quiet my mind and tune in to my intuition. I felt a slight pressure on the center of my forehead.

"Fine. I see an older man standing twenty feet in front of us," I said, wondering if I was making this up.

"And what is he wearing?"

"I don't know, some sort of robe. I think it's blue. He has long hair, blonde or almost white. A crown that sits low on his forehead. Like a... like a..." I fumbled for the word. "It's like a tiara."

We both started giggling.

"Yes," she said. "The Lemurians have come forward to welcome us. Do you see the circle in the trees? It's a meeting place."

"What? No, those are just trees that have fallen, Sara, it's..."

But I broke off in surprise as I realized the fallen trees did indeed form a perfect circle. The tree trunks were massive. It would have been impossible to have arranged them and yet, they were perfectly spaced in circular rows just like an auditorium. We were sitting outside facing the inner circle. Once I saw it, I couldn't believe I *hadn't* seen it before; it was obvious.

"Can't you feel them?" she asked. "They're curious. They aren't quite sure what to make of us."

And I could see them in my mind's eye; it wasn't a clear vision but a quiet knowing. I realized we were looking at their meeting place and I could feel a large circle of beings around us.

"He's saying something about how us visiting the land has brought them new hope that change is coming," I said softly. I felt his approval of our presence. "This is a homecoming of sorts."

"Yes, they are pleased we are here. It's a sign that the surface is changing," she said. After a few minutes of sitting quietly, she added, "They said you are welcome to pick a stone."

I stood up and walked towards the center of the circle, then hesitated. Sara remained seated on the side of the path.

"We weren't supposed to take anything from the forest according to the guidebook," I said. "Are they going to be mad?"

Sara laughed, "they said you can take a rock- they have lots of them. It will remind you of your trip. Go into the center of the circle; they said, 'you're invited'."

I cautiously walked into the center circle. I felt unseen eyes on me as I scanned the ground, unsure of which rock to take. A big one? A small one? A piece of wood? Finally, I picked up a pinkish rock that fit neatly in my palm. I liked the fact it was small enough to carry with me.

"This one," I said, but I secretly second guessed myself. What if they were expecting me to choose a special stone? I put it in my pocket and rejoined her on the path.

We sat in silence, then, after a while, we decided to head back. Sunlight moved through the leaves of the trees, and particles danced in the beams of light, making me think of fairies. There was something mysterious about the forest. I wished I could have stayed in its beauty longer.

Back in the car, I continued to ponder our trip as we drove down the freeway with the California mountains on the horizon. I realized that I would have missed the mystical experience in the woods if I hadn't stopped and listened to my intuition. The hike would've been like any other hike- it was the pause that made it special. I took time to turn inward and listen, which was what allowed the magic to unfold.

Once we returned to Columbus, the magic continued over the next few months. We hosted the first retreat and received positive feedback. I also grew inspired to create a Seven Day Magic Challenge. I wanted to show others how to break free from the monotony of day-to-day life. I shared the idea with Sara, and we developed a weeklong calendar on the website that contained tips and suggestions for how to add more magic to life. One day, I sat at my computer and played with fonts for a social media post, when I remembered Sara's prediction that I would do something in marketing that I loved. *That's exactly what this is*, I thought in wonder. *Imagine that!*

Around that time, I had another visitation dream from Joe but this one was different. In the dream, I was standing by the kitchen table when Joe casually walked in the front door, like he was returning from a day at work. He had on the same outfit as the last dream, with the blue blazer and jeans. He smiled as he came towards me, and I greeted him with a hug. I suddenly pulled back and looked closely at him, in astonishment.

"Wait," I said, in a surprised tone. "I can actually feel you."

I squeezed his arm again and looked perplexed. I knew he had passed away and yet, I felt him just as clearly as if he was physically standing next to me. He gave me a mischievous grin, like he was secretly proud of himself, but he didn't offer an explanation.

I called out to Jonah and Jules, "Kids, come in here. Your dad's here and we can actually feel him!"

I reached out and tightly hugged Joe again, in disbelief. *I can feel you,* I kept thinking, in awe. The kids cheered and ran into the kitchen. They wrapped their arms around our waists and the four of us stood locked in a singular hug. For one shining moment, I had my family back, whole.

Chapter 21

The fall leaves were beginning to change color as I drove the kids to the cemetery for Joe's birthday. The third anniversary of his death had recently passed and so many things had changed in a few short years. The kids, now ages eleven and thirteen, had grown to enjoy visiting the cemetery. We made what was now our traditional stop at Taco Bell and brought along a picnic basket with cupcakes. It was nearing sunset as we arrived and parked on the side of the cemetery road. We set up camping chairs by the large tree and had a picnic dinner while laughing about old memories. We sang Happy Birthday and since there were no other visitors in the cemetery, I took out my phone and played Joe's music playlist. The kids walked around reading the dates on the memorial plaques, while teasing each other. It quickly turned into an impromptu game of tag. Both were laughing as they circled the tree at Joe's memorial. Jonah belted out the lyrics to Joe's favorite song, Under Pressure, by David Bowie, with an amused smile on his face. The next song came on and I went to change it, but Jules stopped me.

"Let's have dance party!" Jules announced. They began dancing around the cemetery and singing loudly to Let It Be by The Beatles.

I watched them for a minute before joining in and dancing. Their joy was contagious and the three of us began spinning circles in the cool evening air. As I turned with my arms extended, the sunset became an orange blur in the distance.

"Let it be, let it be, let it be..." the three of us sang in unison. Jonah stepped side to side while swinging his arms in a silly dance move. I joined in, laughing at how ridiculous we looked.

"Is this the grandpa dance?" I teased him, smiling.

Three years before, I would have never imagined this moment. The last few years felt like they had passed by in the blink of an eye and had been an entire lifetime all at once. I knew Joe was with us, and in that moment, my heart only felt at peace. Watching your loved ones sing and dance at your gravesite on your birthday? Well, I couldn't think of a better way to be celebrated. Suddenly, I heard honking growing louder in the distance. I looked to the sky, already knowing what I'd see before the first silhouette appeared on the horizon. Three geese flew overhead in a V formation. Somehow, it felt as though something had come full circle.

That same month, I unexpectedly ran into Valerie at a Fall wedding. I hadn't seen her since the year of Joe's death. We were one of the first of the guests to arrive at the reception hall. We sat at adjacent tables, and I watched her pretend not to notice me.

Finally, I broke the silence.

"Hi Valerie," I said, carefully watching for her response.

"Oh, Gina, hi! How are you? I didn't see you there!" she said. We made small talk, but I noticed she seemed slightly uncomfortable.

I hadn't been sure what emotion I would feel when I saw her again - this person who had impacted me so profoundly with a simple sentence. As the years had gone by, my anger had gradually softened. Now, sitting at the table, I almost felt a sense of gratitude towards her. *If she had validated Joe's message back then, would I still be where I am today?* In all honesty, I didn't know the answer.

"Gina, so you're a Reiki Practitioner, too?" someone asked from across the table. I felt Valerie's watchful eye as I answered.

"Yes," I said, with a big smile. "I am."

Chapter 22

"Oh, I remember that picture!" I said, as I touched the corner of a photograph tucked neatly into a bulletin board. "It's one of my favorites. That was the pirate ship in Florida when Jonah was four and Jules was two." I smiled at the memory of the trip. "Look at how blue Jonah's eyes were at that age!"

"I keep these to remind me of Joe," Joe's mom said. I turned around and looked in her direction. "It's hard to believe it's been three years," she continued. "Sometimes it feels like much longer to me."

"Yeah, it does feel weird, doesn't it? Sometimes it feels longer to me too. It's a nice memory board. I haven't seen some of these pictures in a long time," I said, as I smiled at her. I could hear the football game from the far room of their house. I knew without looking that Jonah would be sitting side by side on the couch next to Joe's dad; both not speaking and both listening closely to the announcer's commentary on the game. Back in the living room, I sat down on the loveseat and placed an arm around Jules, who was sitting next to me.

"She looks so much like you," she said, glancing at both of us. Jules shifted, suddenly shy. I patted her leg and smiled.

"Do you think? She does resemble me in a lot of ways. People always tell me how much Jonah looks like Joe and I think he secretly likes that."

"Do you think so?" she asked, looking thoughtful.

"Oh yes," I replied. "My brother always says it's not his features, but his facial expressions are very much Joe."

She smiled at the thought and kept gazing at Jules.

"So, are you dating anyone special?" she asked. "Wait, I guess I shouldn't ask that."

"No, it's ok," I said. "I am dating someone. His name's Matt, and he has two kids, similar in age to Jonah and Jules. He lost his wife the year before Joe died."

I glanced over to see her response, but her face remained open, so I continued to explain the story of how Matt and I met.

"Oh, that's wonderful," she said, when I'd finished. I looked at her for a long moment wondering how hard it must be to hear that your deceased child's spouse is in a new relationship. "Are you getting married soon?" she asked.

I paused for a moment, unsure of how to answer. For a long time, all I wanted was to be married again, yet I couldn't deny something inside me was changing. I saw the future with Matt, and it was loving and safe; yet for reasons I couldn't explain, my heart was asking to explore a different path. I was just beginning to investigate those feelings, unsure of how to proceed. I felt like I was in a game show, wanting to tell the host, 'I'd like door #3, please'. But what was behind that door was still completely unknown.

"Oh, I don't think I'll get married again for a long time," I laughed. "Matt's nice though, you'd like him. He's very different from Joe," I added, tentatively. I wondered why

I felt the need to clarify that point, but her face lit up immediately.

"Well, there could be only one Joe," she said, proudly, with
a smile. "He was one of a kind."

I nodded in agreement, then turned to an old photo of Joe,
smiling. My heart filled with warmth as I reflected on how
that teenage boy had grown into the man who became my
husband and shaped the course of my life.

I thought about a message he had recently shared, and
deep in my heart, I knew he would always be with me.

"Yes," I said thoughtfully. "Yes, he really was."

"Remember how much I loved you - that piece still remains."

– Joe

Acknowledgments

W riting this memoir has been a deeply personal and transformative journey, filled with stops and starts along the way. It is a project that could not have been completed without the support of so many incredible people.

First, I want to thank my children, Jonah and Jules, for allowing me to share a part of their life story. As I revisited moments from our past, I was keenly aware that this book represents only one perspective of our shared experiences, and each of you has your own unique version to tell. I hope you both know how deeply you are loved and how proud your dad and I are of you. It's amazing to see the extraordinary young adults you've become.

To Joe: you remain one of the most remarkable people I've ever known. This book is as much about our shared life as it is about my personal journey. Thank you for giving me the courage to tell my version of our story and for standing by me in life and in spirit. I had no idea that

David Bowe's "Under Pressure" would become the theme song for Team Kitzmiller and I love the signs and synchronicities. Keep sending them!

To my family: I hope each of you shines through my writing as brightly as you did in real life. Your unwavering support carried me through the most difficult chapters of my life, and for that, I am endlessly grateful.

To my sister and brother, Holly and Jason: you are truly the best. I couldn't ask for more loyal or caring siblings. You always have my back, and I hope you know how much I appreciate you.

To my parents, Barbara and David Penhorwood, thank you for always being there for me and for the kids. Dad, you never bat an eye when I share something I'm doing (even when it's *way* outside the norm). Your encouragement means the world to me, and I hope you know just how deeply I value and love you. Thank you for always believing in me.

To Joe's family: At the outset of writing this memoir, I struggled with how much to share. My deepest concern was that I might inadvertently hurt your feelings. My hope is that I've struck a balance in telling this story—honoring the extraordinary person Joe was while also reflecting the truths of our marriage. Thank you for your support throughout this journey. As I write this, I am grateful for the connections that remain and hope they continue to grow.

To my 'Mom's Club' friends, Laurel, Deb, Whitney, and Kelley—I know I'm not always the easiest friend to have, as I often get lost in my work or my inner world, but your steadfast support and encouragement have meant everything to me. I couldn't have asked for a more special group of women to lift me up when I felt like I couldn't stand on my own. Thank you for being my lighthouse.

To Jeff Rheinfrank, readers will recognize you as an old friend and medic from the funeral home—but you turned out to be so much more. A soulmate who appeared unexpectedly behind Door #3. I'm so grateful I followed my heart. The joy and laughter you bring into my life are immeasurable. Thank you for your unwavering support in everything I do.

Thank you to Meredith Beardmore for writing the most perfect foreword and for inspiring me to keep going when I felt discouraged. You were the wind beneath this project when I wanted to throw in the towel, and your belief in this book made all the difference.

To Lori Vynalek, thank you for being one of the 'good ones' in the world of energy healers and mediums. I feel like I was meant to sit next to you in that reiki class—you were the best thing to come out of it. Your guidance, wisdom, and laughter have been invaluable.

To Courtney and Nicole—although our friendships formed and grew after this chapter in my life, thank you for being part of my inner circle. Your support means so much to me.

A special thank you to my writing coach and editor, Jo Burns. You took a *very* rough and fragmented first draft and encouraged me to turn it into a cohesive story. Our sessions, your instruction, and your editing made this book so much stronger than I ever thought it could be. I would never have reached the last page without your guidance and support.

I'd also like to thank Lisa Umina for believing in this project and to Elite Voices for providing a platform for my voice to be heard.

To my Guides "The A-Team" and "Nueva Soul" (Team One and Team Two), thank you for your unwavering support. I joke that I must be a challenge because I have such a BIG team around me. A special shout-out to Mr. Rudyard Kipling for his assistance with my writing. My Guides hold a special place in my heart—thank you for walking with me, picking me up when I fall, and holding me steady in all things. In deepest gratitude.

Finally, to the readers who pick up this book—thank you for being part of this journey. I hope my story resonates with you and offers insight into the resilience of the human spirit, the enduring power of love, and the transformative nature of grief. May you find inspiration and the quiet knowing of *I can do this*…because you can.

About the Author

Gina Kitzmiller is the founder and Grand Master of Trimatri Reiki™ and the visionary behind The Karuna Life. As an Intuitive, Reiki Master-Teacher, and Healer, Gina works with clients worldwide, offering compassionate guidance to help them heal deep emotional wounds, release limiting beliefs, and align with their highest potential. She is also the creator of *Trimatri Soul Scribe*™ artwork, which channels soul codes to inspire activation and personal growth.

Certified as a Reiki Master in Usui Reiki Ryoho, Gina is also an Advanced Divine I AM Practitioner and Akashic Records Facilitator. Her extensive credentials include certifications as a grief educator, yoga teacher (RYT 200), breath coach, and Holden Qi Gong instructor (200-hour). With a master's degree in education in rehabilitation counseling, Gina integrates her diverse expertise to offer holistic, soul-centered support.

As a dedicated teacher and mentor, Gina exclusively trains and attunes students to Trimatri Reiki, empowering them to step into their own healing roles with confidence and mastery. Gina also leads *Soul Rise* retreats and online workshops, helping participants cultivate clarity, connection, and personal transformation.

As the host of *The Karuna Life Podcast*, Gina delves into metaphysical and spiritual topics, offering practical tools and inspiration for personal transformation. Her mission is to help others embrace their spiritual gifts, heal deeply, and live in alignment with their soul's purpose.

SOUL WALK

THE UNEXPECTED GIFTS OF GRIEF & CONNECTION TO THOSE IN SPIRIT

a memoir

GINA KITZMILLER

A conversation with Gina Kitzmiller

A conversation with Gina Kitzmiller

Themes and Inspiration

What inspired you to write Soul Walk, and how does the title encapsulate your journey?

The inspiration to write *Soul Walk* began as a love letter to God—a heartfelt way to express my gratitude for the support I felt during the grieving process. I started writing in the summer following Joe's death, but completing the book took several drafts and spanned more than three years. In hindsight, I'm grateful for the time it took. Those years allowed me to process, reflect, and grow, ultimately shaping the book into something much deeper and more meaningful.

In terms of the title, I struggled to come up with the perfect title. Initially, it was called *One Light in the Dark*, but as the story evolved and deepened, the title needed to reflect that growth. I tried a few other titles, but they didn't really resonate. The name *Soul Walk* came to me during meditation, and it just 'clicked.' It truly represents the entire journey—both personal and universal—and my hope is that it conveys the depth and complexity of the themes woven throughout this book.

Storytelling Choices

What moments or experiences were the most challenging to write about, and why?

Writing about the day I received the news that Joe had died, and later cleaning out his apartment, was incredibly difficult. Reliving those moments brought back a flood of emotions, and I often just let myself cry while I worked. When it came time for editing, I found myself stalling, reluctant to revisit the memories.

I also worried about getting the details right. What if I forgot something important, or someone came forward to say my account wasn't accurate? In the end, I had to trust my memories and write the story as I remembered it. I know others might have their own versions of events, and that's okay. I don't claim my account is flawless—these are the details as I recall them, shaped by how the memories formed for me.

Were there personal stories or events that you didn't get to mention?

Yes, there are many stories that I left out for various reasons. Yet there is one story I wish I could've shared…

My best friend from high school, Kristin Darby, is mentioned a few times in this book. She had incredible energy that could captivate an entire room. I met her when I was 15 years old—a pivotal year for me. She sat in front of me in English class, and I immediately knew I wanted her to be my best friend. It wasn't a hard decision—she was smart, beautiful, incredibly funny, and so talented. Kristin had this rare gift of making everyone laugh, often causing the whole room to erupt in laughter. I was thrilled when we became friends, and eventually best friends.

Even after high school, Kristin remained a huge part of my life. We had so much fun in our twenties, staying out late and dancing at bars. She was the kind of person who made every moment brighter and a little more vivid. I remember we were out one night with our friend Susie. And the three of us were in our own world – having drinks, telling old stories and cracking up. A waiter appeared with drinks from a patron. As the man left the restaurant, he paused by our table and said, "I'm not here to bother you, but this whole place has been watching the three of you having so much fun all night - I just wanted to buy a round. Have a good night, ladies."

We talked about how we would get married and be old ladies on a golf course and drinking martinis (Ironically, I don't play golf or drink martinis, but back then it sounded like a solid plan). Yet life didn't turn out as we expected. At age 27, Kristin was unexpectedly diagnosed with lung cancer—a diagnosis that shocked everyone, including her doctors. While I was on the brink of a new chapter with Joe—building a life, getting married, and preparing for motherhood—Kristin was facing the unimaginable. She underwent surgery to remove part of her lung and endured rounds of chemotherapy and radiation.

I wish I could say I was the best friend she needed during that time, but I wasn't. It's one of my deepest regrets. I was young and naïve, and I thought that if I buried my head in the sand, I could somehow protect myself—and her—from the reality of death. I did what many people do: I avoided the elephant in the room. I tiptoed around conversations, terrified of saying the wrong thing and upsetting her. In looking back, I see how I unintentionally left her alone.

If I could go back, I would do so many things differently. I would have had the hard conversations. I would have asked Kristin honest questions about her experience. In the early days after her diagnosis, I tried. Sometimes, I got it 'right.' But as the years passed and the end drew near, I panicked. We felt like two ships passing in the night. My life was just beginning and hers was drawing to a close. So I left the burden of those deeper conversations on her shoulders.

She passed away just two weeks before Jonah was born. When I arrived at the hospital after she passed to say goodbye, the staff rushed over with a wheelchair, assuming I was in labor because of how far along I was in my pregnancy. I remember standing at the threshold of her hospital room, looking at her in that bed, and wanting with every fiber of my being to run away. I didn't want to be there. I didn't know how to react, and I didn't know how to grieve.

I buried those feelings deep inside me, unsure of what else to do. It would be years before I began to process my grief and shame to heal from that experience. She eventually stepped in and helped in spirit, but that's a story I hope makes it into a future book.

Healing and Resilience

What tools or practices were most instrumental in your journey through grief?

I'm a big fan of Dr. Alan Wolfelt, whose books on grief—especially those addressing grief after suicide—were a lifeline in the weeks following Joe's death. His words were filled with kindness and understanding. I hope to meet him one day to thank him in person and give him a heartfelt hug.

Journaling, guided meditation, and automatic writing were also instrumental in helping me process my grief. These practices provided a space for me to explore my emotions, find clarity, and begin to heal.

Spiritual and Philosophical Reflections

Are there any symbolic or metaphorical elements you hope readers will notice?

Yes, one element that might not be immediately obvious is how the visitation dreams evolved over time. As I progressed in my own healing, the details of Joe's visitation dreams grew more vivid and meaningful. I didn't fully realize the symbolism until after the book was complete, but it feels like an important reflection of my journey.

Connecting with Readers

Many readers may find comfort in your story. What do you hope they take away about the nature of grief?

I hope readers see that grief isn't just one thing—it's many things. It's pain and sorrow, yes, but it's also love, joy, and transformation. My intention was to show the multifaceted nature of grief and how, even in its depths, it can hold moments of light and growth.

I also hope my story inspires readers to embark on their own journeys of self-exploration, particularly when it comes to the "narrative" of loss. By gently questioning deeply held emotions and beliefs—like "I'm all alone" or "they're no longer with me"—I hope they can arrive at their own truths.

My wish is that these explorations lead them to greater peace and understanding.

If a reader is currently navigating grief, is there one piece of advice or encouragement you'd share?

I want them to know that their loved ones are still with them in spirit. You don't need to be an intuitive or a medium to connect with those who have passed; they hear you when you speak to them and are aware of what's happening in your life. While the relationship may no longer exist in the physical sense, it can still be deeply meaningful and supportive.

I encourage creating a new kind of connection with loved ones in spirit. Include them in your life in ways that feel right to you—set a place for them at dinner, share a cup of coffee in the morning, or simply speak to them in quiet moments. These gestures can be profoundly healing, reinforcing the inner knowing that the bonds of love transcend death and never truly fade away.

Personal Reflections

Where are you now in your journey, both personally and emotionally, since the events of Soul Walk?

My life has transformed in so many ways since the events of *Soul Walk*. It's hard to believe that this year marks the seventh anniversary of Joe's passing. Time feels paradoxical—like it's been both a year and a decade since that day. Oddly, the passage of years brings its own sadness for me. Grief, I've learned, doesn't have a finish line. It remains like a quiet tide in my heart, ever-present but no longer overwhelming.

Today, Jeff and I live in Columbus, Ohio, with our children and our three dogs: Max, Benny, and Eddie George. Jonah and Jules are now teenagers, which feels surreal. The years seem to fly by and watching them grow has been both beautiful and bittersweet.

Life is full, though it looks very different than it did seven years ago. The journey has shaped me in ways I never could have imagined. I hope it's made me a kinder, more compassionate person. It's also taught me the importance of following my dreams and embracing my own truth—a lesson I carry with me every day.

Let's Connect!

I'd love to hear from you and be part of your journey. Visit www.thekarunalife.com to explore heart-centered living, energy healing, and upcoming events. For insights into Trimatri Reiki™ and training opportunities, head over to www.trimatrihealing.com. You can also tune in to *The Karuna Life Podcast* for inspiring conversations on intuition, healing, and spiritual growth—available on your favorite platforms.

Don't forget to follow me on Instagram @thekarunalife for weekly messages, inspiration, and updates. Have questions or want to schedule a session? Feel free to email me at gina@thekarunalife.com. I can't wait to connect with you!

www.ingramcontent.com/pod-product-compliance
Lightning Source LLC
Chambersburg PA
CBHW070839100426
42813CB00003B/684